The Breast Cancer
JOURNEY

Stories of Hope with
Action Items for Survival

Lucinda C. West
and
Pamela J. Schlembach

WESTBOW
PRESS®
A DIVISION OF THOMAS NELSON
& ZONDERVAN

Scripture taken from the Holy Bible, NEW INTERNATIONAL VERSION®. Copyright © 1973, 1978, 1984 by Biblica, Inc. All rights reserved worldwide. Used by permission. NEW INTERNATIONAL VERSION® and NIV® are registered trademarks of Biblica, Inc. Use of either trademark for the offering of goods or services requires the prior written consent of Biblica US, Inc.

WestBow Press books may be ordered through booksellers or by contacting:

WestBow Press
A Division of Thomas Nelson & Zondervan
1663 Liberty Drive
Bloomington, IN 47403
www.westbowpress.com
1 (866) 928-1240

ISBN: 978-1-5127-2993-1 (sc)
ISBN: 978-1-5127-2992-4 (e)

Library of Congress Control Number: 2016902052

Print information available on the last page.

WestBow Press rev. date: 3/11/2016

Contents

Dedication

 *Lucinda West*

My mother always provided me with a spirit of adventure. She encouraged me to never give up, no matter how difficult the journey may seem. She also instilled in me a great love for Jesus. He was her best friend, and she spent the last 30+ years of her life in Christian ministry. When her physicians told her there was nothing more they could do to stop the aggressive melanoma, and she was at the end of life, she responded with a smile on her face: "I get to go be with my Jesus." This book is for you, mom.

 Pamela Schlembach

I dedicate this book to all the wonderful patients, families and Breast Friends members I have met over the years as an oncologist. Your grace, strength and gratitude inspire me daily.

> *"I pray that God, who gives hope, will bless you*
> *with complete happiness and peace*
> *because of your faith. And may the power of*
> *the Holy Spirit fill you with hope."*
> *Romans 15:13 (CEV)*

Preface

Sharing your story is therapeutic. Allowing yourself for a few moments to be vulnerable develops character and strength in you. Passing your story on for the sake of helping another builds bridges between you and others. Knowing that you have the capability to influence another's frame of mind increases confidence for finding solutions to your own situation.

The contributors in this book have openly shared stories from their hearts as a means to help others who are going through a similar trial in the breast cancer journey. They have passed on their stories to you, the reader, anxious to share messages of hope and encouragement. Many privately shared with me that this process of writing down their story and sharing it with you was therapeutic for them. We thank you, our dear reader, for accepting this book and reading it. Our desire is that your life will be enriched as you go through this difficulty journey—that you will experience hope. And we thank you for passing it on as you mentor others who come after you.

A friend who had successfully battled breast cancer passed on a devotional book to me once I had been diagnosed with the same disease[1]. She read it from cover to cover while recovering from her double mastectomy. A friend of hers had passed it on to her, and who knows where it started before that. This pink, little 90-day devotional with inspirational messages from women who had battled different types of cancer had made its way to my hands because someone cared enough to mail it to me. The women in this book shared Scripture, words of encouragement, and a prayer. It meant so much to me that my friend had the foresight and initiative to pass it on.

I recognized some of the names. Some had lost their battle since writing their piece, while others were still thriving.

On day 45 of the devotional, I realized that my friend, as well as many of the women who wrote their stories, were further along in their journey than I was at that moment. Cancer-free, their battle was over; they were survivors. Even those who "lost" the battle did not see it as a loss. For to them, to die was a gain (Philippians 1:21). As I read the day's devotional, titled *The Eternal Now*, I was energized by the thought that one day I too would be a survivor and cancer-free.

My devotional book was unmarked—good as new. There were no notes in the margins. The binding was in great shape. Nothing was underlined, highlighted, or marked. No name designated its owner. Pages were not dog-eared. I too refrained from underlining or highlighting meaningful thoughts in order to present my future friend with a preserved copy of the book, in the same way my friend did for me. On the day it arrived in the mail, I made a plan to pass it on after I finished. I didn't know who that would be, and I would let God lead me when the time was right.

Fast-forward one year after my mastectomy. I was attending a support group for breast cancer patients and survivors when Dr. Pamela Schlembach (lovingly called "Dr. Pam," the facilitator of the group) gave the night to all the ladies in the room. It was an open microphone to share your personal story of hope to one another. She stressed, "We already know the bad. So, tell us what you did to find hope, peace, and strength to help others in this room." One by one, women filed forward to share her story, each as unique as the woman who shared it. We laughed, we cried, and we said "aha" as we listened to stories of hope and great expectation. I took the little book with me to the front of the room and shared my story with this group of women for the first time (I cried all the way through it). Afterward, I passed on the book to another newly diagnosed woman. Sharing my story and sharing the book was therapeutic for me, as well as many other women in attendance that night.

On the way out as I helped Dr. Pam carry the left over donated cupcakes, I said to her, "Wouldn't it be great if we could put all these stories together into a book?" She agreed and liked the idea. Dr. Pam and I wanted to provide other women with the opportunity to experience the same inspirational messages we had witnessed that evening, as well as on other occasions. We had so much to share; the walls could not contain all the messages. We talked more about the great night and decided to get together over lunch to discuss this big adventure of writing a book to help others.

This is how the book *The Breast Cancer Journey: Stories of Hope with Actions for Survival* came to be. Over a fine lunch and stimulating conversation we pressed forward with a decision to publish a book, and agreed to donate the net proceeds of this project to further cancer research. We couldn't wait to pass it on!

About the Book Editors

 **Lucinda C. West, Ph.D.** was diagnosed at the age of 49 with Stage III, triple positive, invasive right breast cancer. She was subsequently treated at MD Anderson Cancer Center located in The Woodlands, Texas. Her treatment included six months of neoadjuvant chemotherapy, a modified radical right mastectomy, 33 daily radiation treatments, followed by eventual reconstruction. She is cancer-free.

Dr. West earned her Ph.D. from Regent University. She is a Licensed Marriage and Family Therapist in Texas (LMFT-S) and Florida (LMFT), and a Licensed Mental Health Counselor (LMHC) in the state of Florida. She serves as Faculty Chair and Program Director for the dually accredited (COAMFTE and CACREP) Marriage and Family Counseling/Therapy program at Capella University. She has more than 20 years of experience providing marriage, family, and couples therapy, teaching master's level MFT and CES doctoral students, in addition to supervising master's level clinicians for licensure. Dr. West is a Clinical Fellow in the American Association for Marriage and Family Therapy (AAMFT), an AAMFT Approved Supervisor and a professional member of the American Counseling Association (ACA).

She has been married to her husband for 30 years. They have two grown children, one grandchild, and a dog. Hobbies include road trips on the Harley Davidson, spending time with the family, and playing with her new grandbaby. In addition she loves to sing, play the keyboard, and watch bluebirds nest in their Texan backyard.

 **Pamela J. Schlembach M.D.,** is a board certified radiation oncologist and holds an academic appointment as Professor in the Department of Radiation Oncology at the University of Texas, MD Anderson. Her regional office is conveniently located in The Woodlands, Texas, where she has been serving Montgomery county residents full-time since 2004.

Dr. Schlembach received her medical degree from the Medical College of Ohio in Toledo and completed her residency in radiation oncology at the world-renowned MD Anderson Cancer Center in 2002 where she joined the faculty. She is a pioneer in the outreach program and is responsible for formulating the first multidisciplinary team for MD Anderson in breast cancer in a community setting. She serves as a community liaison for MD Anderson and speaks at a multitude of educational events and donates countless hours to education and support. She is the medical director of the Gamma Knife program at CHI St. Luke's Woodlands hospital. She also facilitates "Breast Friends," the largest breast cancer support and survivorship group in Montgomery County. She has received numerous publications and awards.

She has been married for 38 years and has two adult children. She enjoys cooking, biking and entertaining friends and family.

Acknowledgements

First and foremost I give glory to Jesus Christ, our Lord and Savior, for healing me of breast cancer. Our lives are in His hands and His will. His guidance led me to the wonderful treatment I received at MD Anderson. It is there I met some amazing lifelong friends through whose hands He worked miracles.

In addition, we want to thank the ladies who took time out of their busy schedules and contributed to this book. Revisiting the journey was challenging at times. Their private emails and conversations revealed many tears were shed when writing their stories. Yet they saw the vision for helping others who would suffer a diagnosis of breast cancer in the future. Breast Friends, your "atta girl" comments encouraged us to hang in there and finish pulling this project together. We could not have done this without you!

My family is my greatest ally and I want to acknowledge their role. When the imposter syndrome snuck in and tried to steal my confidence, they offered counterattacks. West family, I love you all to the moon and back!

We also want to thank the following friends who read and edited stories, provided constructive criticism on how to format the stories more effectively, and gave encouraging comments for completing this project. Jena Mayo, you are my best friend for life, and I owe you for all the creative elements you added to this book! Robert Schlembach, your direct approach as a copy editor sharpened our skills and made us much stronger writers. Thank you both for your tireless efforts to ensure our grammar and punctuation were spot-on!

Introduction:
How to Use This Book

This book is a compilation of stories written by women who have been touched by breast cancer. They come from unique personalities, a variety of ages and stages, different treatment modalities, and multiple perspectives.

One way to read this book is the traditional way – from beginning to end. Or, you may choose to skip around and read the stories that best relate to you at the present moment. For example, if you are going through chemotherapy, you might read a story about chemotherapy. Put your mark on the stories, as you read them, so you can go back and revisit your favorites or easily locate the ones you have not yet read. Or you may decide to start with those stories containing your favorite Scriptures. We encourage you to begin each day of your journey by reading one story and reflecting on how you are feeling that day. Each day's reading is divided into four parts, further described below.

My Story. Word spread quickly and women across the nation were eager to contribute. Each story begins with the contributing author sharing a moment in her[2] journey. Some authors contributed more than one moment, from different points in the journey. This book is a collection from survivors as well as those still battling breast cancer. Some have written satirically, while others shoot straight from the hip. We intentionally kept the different approaches so you could hear the voice and sense the heart of each author as you read. We wanted our readers to witness their personalities firsthand with a profound and absorbing interest.

The women represented in this book come from all walks of life; cancer does not discriminate. Some were very young when they were diagnosed; others were older. Many have embraced a spiritual faith as evidenced in their words and Scriptural references. Some writers like Cherie and Tanya have found humor in their situations, and we invite you to laugh with them. Other stories are more touching and require tissues. You will meet Noreta who embraced the pink, and Rachel who despised it. Some were diagnosed very early in stage zero or one; while others were diagnosed stage four, experience chronic cancer, or have recurring cancer. Some have been cancer-free for years; others have been recently deemed cancer-free. We hope you connect with the various authors of these stories as they have shared a part of their journey so openly.

A common thread is woven throughout the stories contained in this book: the message of hope.

How I Got Through It. In this section each author will share how she got through the moment in her journey about which you have just read. Each story provides a message of inspiration, survival and an eternal life where one day we may all pass to a cancer-free place. As you read each story, ponder how you can relate, wherever you are in your cancer journey. This section provides words of encouragement to help you persevere. One thing we all have in common, and this is what brings us together as "breast friends."

Action Items. An action item challenges readers to do something, to mobilize the body, mind, and spirit. Each story contains at least one action item, and sometimes more than one option is presented. The reader is encouraged to take a moment each morning, and then take action. It is intensely difficult to hear the word "cancer." Yet we must not let it seize our day. Take action today, and vow to make each day a good one.

Yearbook. A "Yearbook" page follows each story and action item. Yearbooks are memory books. They remind of experiences we have had, and provide a commentary on our relationships with others. *You now belong to a club* in this university called life, and this is a memoir of our journey together. This is a section where you, the reader, can reflect on the action item or write a note about your experience on that particular day. Whether you are feeling sick, healthy, sad, or encouraged, journal it! Or perhaps you would like to reply to the story you just read, asking a rhetorical question or adding to it. Express what you feel, even if you can only muster the energy to write one word.

This book yearns to be written in. Mark it. Highlight it. Underline key phrases. Dog-ear your favorite stories. Draw a picture. Put your name in it. Write in it! Whatever your comfort level, just do it! Journaling is good for the soul. You may want to include a song lyric, Scripture or quote that supports you in that moment of time, or just draw a symbol or number on a scale of 1-10 representing your feeling. As you read each day and consider your own experiences, discover something to look forward to.

Pass It On. When you have finished, you are encouraged to pass on this book to a friend, neighbor, or family member who is starting her breast cancer journey. You may purchase a new one if you want to keep your own Yearbook to revisit your notes from time to time, or you may decide to pass this one on as you have now become a co-author in this Yearbook of life. We hope you will find strength and encouragement as we travel this journey together.

Cancer Doesn't Deserve a Song

Cathy Donaldson

"By day the Lord commands his steadfast
love, and at night his song is with me, a prayer
to the God of my life." ~Psalm 42:8

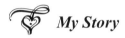 ***My Story***

Off to the side of an atrium at MD Anderson, tucked behind a large pillar, sits a grand piano. Its glossy black-and-white shines incongruous in a visual ocean of soothing, matte, earth tones.

After a particularly difficult appointment that ended long after most people were gone for the day, I stopped abruptly and asked my husband to play for me. He drew up the piano bench. I pulled close a chair. He played. I cried. He fudged the tricky bits of my favorite song. I laughed, tears running into my mouth. He slaughtered a very nice Chopin piece. I breathed in deep; a shimmer of a glimpse of what God sees in him. He played on, unaware. I fell in love with him all over again—captivated, pierced.

This afternoon, he gave an encore. It was earlier than the last time, (the building still full of people). So many people smiled as they walked past his musical rendition. Some nodded at me from their wheelchairs, tired eyes peering from hairless heads wrapped in fabric. My heart ached like last time, but this time my cheeks stayed dry.

My husband played all the usuals. Then he started improvising, which always makes us both laugh because he is not great at it! He played for a minute, paused, then played a few measures at a time and began narrating his music. More laughter. Mostly silly narration like what the song sounds like during (ahem) a difficult time of the month for me. What the song sounds like when that time of the month is over. What the song sounds like when our baby toddles into the room. He said several others, but I was too busy laughing to remember now what they were. Then, I asked him what cancer sounds like.

Silence.

He turned and looked at me square in the eyes and said quietly, "Cancer doesn't deserve a song." Then he turned back to the piano and played a little more, but truth be told, I cannot remember that either because my ears were too full of what he had just said. "Cancer doesn't deserve a song." Words as black and white as the keys under his fingers.

 *How I Got Through It*

Oh how I wish we had the luxury of black-and-white in the decision-making arena. Every decision we face is about as gray as they come. A perfect storm of events creating an overcast scenario that just won't dissipate. Where is the sun? Where is the Son? I blew a fuse and just could not get quiet in my head. My soul felt that feeling you get when the wind is knocked out of you. I knew in my brain that I'd be able to "soul-breathe" again, but I just couldn't draw it in on my own. So my husband checked us into a hotel and promised me the time I needed to get my wind back. Forty hours and twenty pages of my scribbly handwriting later, we checked out. I would like to say I was refreshed, but I wasn't.

Actually, I was more tired than when we checked in, but my soul was breathing again.

Action Items

When life's "gray" seems to be overtaking you, what is your response? Take a moment to articulate your thoughts in the Yearbook page below.

Yearbook

Can't Complain

Pamela Schlembach

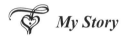 *My Story*

My story is found in a patient who became my friend, then became a patient again. She taught me a lifelong lesson about maintaining a positive attitude. I first met Vicky in 1983 at the University of Toledo. She had a history of Hodgkin's lymphoma diagnosed eight years earlier at the age of 19. At the time of her initial diagnosis, she was in respiratory failure. Her doctors were not very hopeful she would live due to her extensive disease, but she became one of the first patients in Toledo treated with a new life-saving technology. After months of therapy she was cured.

At our first encounter, I was impressed by how upbeat and peaceful she was. We became fast friends after that day. I was a nuclear medicine technologist at the time and Vicky was the first young cancer survivor I had met. Over the years, no matter what challenges were going on in her life, she would give the same answer to my standard question: "How are you?" She would say, "I can't complain. I'm alive and God is good." I always loved her zeal for life, strong faith and positive attitude.

She experienced infertility from her radiation treatment in the early 1980's. To everyone's surprise, she later became pregnant. Eventually, she was the mother of three boys in the 1990's. Vicky had a lifelong dream to adopt a daughter from China. She eventually adopted two daughters. I too had a lifelong dream to become a doctor and entered medical school at the age of 34. We stayed close and shared our victories and challenges.

In 1998, I moved away to Houston, Texas to begin my residency in radiation oncology at MD Anderson Cancer Center. Life was wonderfully hectic but I stayed in close contact with Vicky through frequent short phone calls. During my residency, an article was published about the toxicities associated with radiation treatment in young patients who had been treated for Hodgkin's lymphoma in the 1970's and 1980's. These young women developed breast cancer 20 to 30 years later in the areas of the radiation treatment fields. As the data was being presented, I realized Vicky fell into this category and contacted her about this new published information. Her response to the news was remarkable. "If it had not been for that treatment, I would have died. I can't complain." Impressive response, I thought. Not a lawsuit or anger—only gratitude.

When Vicky found out she had breast cancer, she bravely said to me, "Now I know why God has directed your steps into oncology and why you are at the top cancer center in the United States. It was for me." We both cried. She and I would visit briefly after each daily radiation treatment and I would ask how she was. Without fail she would say, "I can't complain. I'm at the best place for cancer and with my best friend."

In 2010, Vicky was diagnosed with cystic mucoepidermoid carcinoma of the parotid gland. Under skillful hands, she came away cancer free and with no facial deficits. Again I asked how are you. "I can't complain! I am cancer free and so glad I know people in high places." She even laughed.

To date, Vicky has esophageal strictures, neck atrophy, lymphedema, developed squamous cell cancer in her lateral chest wall, and is not a candidate for reconstruction due to her prior treatments, and yet I have never seen her bitter or angry about what she has gone through medically. I called her while I was writing this story about her life and shared her impact on me, again asking, "How are you today?"

She replied, "Can't complain. We are all upright." We both laughed, and I was once again reminded of how grateful I am to know this amazing woman.

How I Got Through It

Vicky has been through so much and yet she remains so positive. She has reminded me on numerous occasions that she is grateful God directed our steps to each other. She has shared with me how thankful she is that I pursued a career in oncology and aided in her cancer care. The truth be told, I need her in my life. Her calm response and grace in the face of a multitude of medical issues seems to help me to do my job day after day. She has an insatiable will to live life to the fullest despite all her medical setbacks. I think of her often as I work in my oncology clinic. Her strength gives me hope and drive to treat my cancer patients.

Action Items

Imagine your friend has just called you on the phone, asking you, "How are you today?" How might you respond with a positive attitude? Finish this sentence: "I can't complain, and here is why..." Write your thoughts in the Yearbook page that follows.

Yearbook

Lavender Sacrifice

Cindy Murray

*"Then Mary took a twelve-ounce jar of expensive
perfume made from essence of nard, and she anointed
Jesus' feet with it, wiping his feet with her hair. The
house was filled with the fragrance." ~John 12:3 (NLT)*

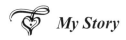 *My Story*

Selling my lavender business may have saved my life. This was a small price to pay as I look back at the events that occurred that year. When my husband was transferred to Houston, I closed the company, which had previously run 24-7 making lavender soaps, lotions, and potions. It was a tough decision, but one I have not regretted. Before the move, I completed my annual well woman tests in Canada. No problems. All clear.

About seven months later my husband was on a business trip to Brazil, and I had a habit of sleeping on his side of the bed while he was gone. I felt a lump in my breast the size of a golf ball. I kept it to myself. In an instant my life was changed. I went from lavender relaxation to fear and agitation. Things happened extremely fast after that.

The same weekend I received a call from my mother that my father had passed away. Preoccupied with making plans to fly home, that little voice in the back of my head kept nagging me. *"Go to the doctor."* It's amazing how fast the system works in the U.S.A., compared to Canada where I came from. I think I am alive today because I was in the States. After the exam, he scheduled tests for the next day. I objected, "I really need to get home. I'm the only daughter."

I had stage IIIC breast cancer, HER2+. It was very aggressive and serious. They didn't want me to go home, but conceded when I agreed to come back the following Tuesday to discuss treatment. So I went home for a whirlwind trip over the weekend, attended my father's funeral, and then came straight back. I was lucky enough to be in Houston and have the best doctors. I knew God was with me the whole journey. The results from the treatment and surgery were amazing. I believe a miracle happened to me.

How I Got Through It

When Mary doused the feet of Jesus with an expensive perfume, she chose the scent of lavender. I can imagine what the aroma was like throughout the house! Her act represented a total sacrifice, to serve and follow Christ. Through this journey I, too, have learned to sacrifice my own desires and totally rely on God. He performed many miracles in my life, and I started a miracle book to keep track of them all. God has blessed me with a cancer-free life for five years now. Being diagnosed with breast cancer does not have to carry a death sentence. I made pink cupcakes to celebrate the anniversary, and I continue to thank God for His healing and sacrifice my life to serve Him daily.

 *Action Items*

My family was still in Canada. My father had just passed away. My husband was out of the country. Yet, the strength of my family and friends got me through it. There are such kind people in the world, and if you let them they will surprise you with their kindness. Ask God to open your eyes to the kindness of those around you. Make a list of things your friends can do when they come over. Write these ideas in the Yearbook page that follows. They can help, and they want to help! The positive vibrations you get from your friends, and their well wishes will give you strength. Perhaps someone will even draw you a fresh lavender-scented bath.

Yearbook

Shock Can Be a Good Thing

Lucinda West

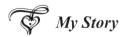 *My Story*

In my early 40s, I had six biopsies, three in each breast. They were all fluid-filled cysts, and as it turned out, nothing to worry about. But this time it was different. I sensed it from the first time I noticed the lump. The mass was solid, and it grew fast.

Redness and pain prompted me to visit my primary care physician to check it out. She ordered a diagnostic mammogram and ultrasound. It appeared that I had a cluster of cysts, or a "benign tumor." She assured me it was nothing to be concerned about, but I should come back in six months just to be sure.

Five months later, I went in for the recommended follow-up ultrasound. As I waited to be called back for the procedure, the medical technicians checked on me several times. They seemed overly attentive. The radiologist found something "suspicious" and recommended a biopsy. The tests revealed a mass that grew from "undetected" to a tumor measuring nine centimeters in size just a few months later. Another ten millimeter mass was found on the lymph node. The radiologist had a concerned look on his face when he did the procedure. He said he would put a rush on the pathology report, even though it sometimes takes ten days to come back.

My doctor called, letting me know the pathology report was back. She wanted me to come in so we could talk for a few minutes. Hmmm. Sounds serious. "Should I bring my husband?" I turned around and picked him up, so we could receive the news together.

The ladies up front didn't even ask for my name; they knew who I was the moment I walked in. They went straight to the doctor to let her know I was there; the wait was brief. She sat down in front of me and looked me straight in the eyes. "You have breast cancer," she said, matter-of-fact. It was in the mass as well as the lymph nodes. A tumultuous rush of sensations followed. Even though we suspected it would be cancer, we were both in shock.

How I Got Through It

A friend told me "shock is a good thing." Our bodies have an incredible defense system to protect us in times of crisis, without immediately feeling the pain associated with bad news. The shock did wear off, and I knew I needed to take action since our lives would be taking a detour for the next several months.

I decided to start blogging. It didn't matter to me if no one read my journey. It would probably be therapeutic for me to write it anyway, I reasoned. Much to my surprise, people did read my blog. Some readers left comments with words of encouragement, others sent text messages, and some called. Prayers and words of support gave me daily doses of strength. It was like vitamins for the soul. I soon discovered that women who read my blog were learning from my experiences. What I thought was helping me was in reality helping others. This, in turn, helped me to get through it once the initial shock wore off.

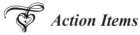 *Action Items*

If you don't already have one, purchase a journal (or use the yearbook pages in this book) and start writing about your experiences. Note every day events, symptoms, feelings, and thoughts, or questions that loom in your mind as you progress through your journey. Keep these notes with you when you go to the doctor and refer to them as needed. Remember to include ways you got through it!

Yearbook

Complete Control

Marlene Shurell

"Nothing can stop the woman with the right mental attitude from achieving her goal; nothing on earth can help the woman with the wrong mental attitude." ~Thomas Jefferson (paraphrased)

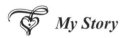 *My Story*

I was hoping for the reassuring "free pass," not at all expecting the call I received. Three days before, I had found a lump in my breast and immediately scheduled a 3-D mammogram. When I first heard the words from the pathologist, "breast carcinoma," there was a sense as though these words could not be real, could not possibly be true, and could not pertain to me. I had never had a major illness. No one in my family had ever had breast cancer. And I actually had protective factors against getting breast cancer. In fact, as I later learned, the only major risk factors that seemed to apply to me were being female and getting older every year! Also uncharacteristic for me, it didn't take long to break down in tears of fear as the word "cancer" rocked around in my head.

The next few weeks and months were a blur of appointments, tests, surgery, follow-up treatments, making decisions within days that would affect the rest of my life, and even realizing that the rest of my life as I had envisioned it would be very different. Blended through it all were many emotions and eye opening realizations, grasping that I was loved and appreciated in ways

I never knew before. I was grateful because in spite of feeling a decrease in my activity level, I was still healthy overall.

How I Got Through It

Through it all, a clarity and distinction came between those things I could control and those things I couldn't. Things I just had to accept as different, and things that remained constant. Changes were multidimensional encompassing physical, emotional, spiritual, and social realms; change included plans for the future as well as plans for the next twenty minutes. But what I knew for sure is that the one thing I had complete control over and could change, shape, treasure and shine out to the world was my attitude. No one could take that away, and no one could tell me how it had to be.

I realized that I could choose to live each moment on my own terms. I know that I have only so long to live, just as each of us (diagnosed or not), has only so long to live. I knew I could choose to live it feeling miserable, angry, feeling sorry for myself or bemoaning my fate. Or I could choose to live, for as long as I have, with joy, appreciation for the moment, aware of opportunities to reach out to others, and looking for opportunities to laugh and love the life I have left. This I know for sure—no one can take my attitude from me. I have complete control over it, and it can make me feel blessed. It fills me with joy and strength for each new day. It belongs to me.

 *Action Items*

Think about your attitude, the one thing you can control. Do you choose to feel sorry for yourself, or do you choose to live life filled with joy while appreciating each moment? In the Yearbook page that follows, write the words "I choose…" and then list the positive mental attitudes you choose to possess from this day forward.

Yearbook

A Bond Between Mother
and Daughter

Tara Latta

"Peace is the result of retraining your mind
to process life as it is, rather than as you
think it should be." ~Wayne Dwyer[3]

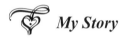 ## *My Story*

It was heart crushing when I thought of the possibility that my 5-year old daughter could be left without a mother; I was diagnosed with breast cancer at the age of 34. Next the questions emerged. When and where would I tell her, and to what depth should I explain my situation? How much information can a 5-year old handle? On the other hand, the big question of whether to tell or not to tell my daughter was not a difficult decision. I knew she needed to know why my physical appearance was going to change, and I wanted to make sure she would see me embrace it and demonstrate acceptance.

I overcame the fear of dying when I realized God already has His plan for my life. Then I could focus on how to tell my family about my cancer. When we did finally sit down to converse, it felt very natural. Gauging from my daughter's expressions while we talked gave me clues for how much to tell her. I was utterly surprised how much she understood. I was amazed at her curiosity. She wanted to understand why my body was physically changing; including losing my hair, losing my breast, nails falling off, and a constant runny nose. My decision to be open and honest with my daughter ended up being an unexpected part of my healing process; she showed me the genuine love through a child's eyes.

How I Got Through It

I chose to be open with my daughter about my cancer, but I tried not to let it change her world. I kept her on a normal schedule even though mine varied from day to day. By the age of six, she had to understand terminology like cancer, hair loss, mastectomy, radiation, ports, wig, and chemo. Like a trooper she absorbed it all, took it in stride and stood by my side. Having my daughter understand what I was going through helped us bond. She tended to my wounds, helped pull out my hair, read me stories, and rubbed my bald head. She was always proud of me and was never afraid to share with friends and teachers about our journey. I am proud to be her Mom!

Action Items

My advice to women with small children is to be proactive. Don't wait until your children see the changes taking place to explain it to them. Let them know there will be a change, and help them understand in advance what they can expect. Keep a positive mental attitude and answer their questions as they come. In the Yearbook page below, note two or three ways you might share your story with your children or one other family member.

Yearbook

Seeds

Rowena Hayes

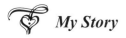 *My Story*

When telling me I had breast cancer the doctor said, "I promise this will not be what takes you out of this world." This immediately gave me hope for my future.

I prayed about what treatment I should choose. It was an interesting concept to me that I had the ability to decide for myself, which treatment I wanted. I prayed for strength and peace for my time of treatment. Part of my treatment involved radiation.

During each radiation session, I noticed that my time for the actual delivery of radiation was always six minutes. Through research I learned that the time for this treatment could vary, so I became curious. After several days of treatment, I questioned the technician. What I was told was just amazing to me. The time of radiation is dependent on nothing more than the age of the radioactive *seed* placed in the machine. Nothing more, nothing less was a factor.

In the Bible there is a story about a mustard seed, the tiniest of seeds. We only need that small amount of a faith for God to work miracles in our life. My faith was tried and tested. My peace and joy were threatened. But, seeds of faith did fall on me, and have forever changed how I view those inevitable valleys in this life. The seeds gave me my life back.

How I Got Through It

I found that little seeds of encouragement brightened my day and my outlook throughout my treatment. Cards helped me, and arrived almost daily in my mailbox. Because of those seeds, I started a ministry, "Whispers of Love," to provide handmade cards to those diagnosed with cancer. It has blessed me so much to provide encouragement to others with just a simple card.

 ## *Action Items*

Purchase some seeds and plant them in some topsoil, inside or outside, depending on the weather and climate at the time you read this. Watch as the seeds burst into new life, and enjoy the growth that comes as a result. If you were writing a card to a friend diagnosed with cancer to provide her with hope and seeds of encouragement, what would it say? Write these thoughts in the Yearbook page that follows, and then receive these words as a means of self-encouragement.

Yearbook

_____

_____

_____

_____

_____

_____

_____

_____

_____

_____

_____

_____

_____

_____

_____

_____

_____

_____

_____

_____

_____

_____

_____

_____

_____

_____

_____

_____

_____

_____

_____

_____

_____

Chemo and Life

Lucinda West

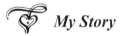 *My Story*

In the very first visit, my medical oncologist told me, "We schedule chemo around your life, not the other way around." That's a great perspective for someone to hear who is newly diagnosed with breast cancer. With this "permission," we took a quick trip to Florida over the Christmas holiday while we had a week between doctor's visits.

We believed the trip to visit friends and family could provide us added strength to endure the upcoming journey. Hugs and tears were shared as we embraced and prayed for one another. It was great seeing all of our friends who crossed our path on that memorable holiday trip. Visiting my mother provided me with additional encouragement.

Lifelong friends hosted us the first few days, insisting we stay in their master suite. They welcomed us with a cozy fire on a cold winter's night. The next morning, our friends made potato pancakes for breakfast and squeezed fresh orange juice from fruit right off their tree. The morning and sunset views over the lake made us thankful to be alive, and life felt "normal." God's artistry was evident to us that day.

A tiny tree with twinkling lights adorned the hotel suite where we lodged for the second half of our trip. No matter where our family travels, we embrace the spirit of Christmas. Eggnog, ham, pumpkin pie, Christmas movies, as well as eating Asian food on Christmas Eve, helped to give our fill of some of our typical family traditions. I was gifted with pink items, new clothes, and hats from my mother to keep me warm during upcoming chemotherapy. We are blessed with children who don't require much to be surprised and satisfied. It was a good holiday, and the cloud of cancer dissipated for a few days.

 ## *How I Got Through It*

Despite what my oncologist told me about scheduling chemotherapy around life, I knew I would need to make room in my week for chemotherapy once we got back home from our trip. I was a very busy professional, wife, and mother. Every minute and day was booked solid. Rather than viewing this as an interruption, however, I captured the opportunity to evaluate all the activities on my calendar. Work, play, and family were prioritized to only include those things that really mattered. This was a God-given chance for me to let go of all the extracurricular activities on my schedule. I learned to say "no" to the extra opportunities for additional income, and I made a commitment to take time daily for myself, and my family.

 ## *Action Items*

Don't allow your cancer treatment to rule your life. Life should not revolve around your treatment schedule. Live life and press on! Take time for you, your family, and the most important things in life. Remember this is but a temporary inconvenience. Record your thoughts about priorities in the Yearbook page that follows.

Yearbook

1984

Patti Wolford

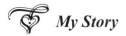 *My Story*

When I was a teenager, George Orwell's book *Nineteen Eighty Four* was required reading. From that time on I wondered what I would be doing that year. When 1984 finally rolled around I was 33 years old; I had been married fourteen years to a wonderful man, and I had two handsome sons ages seven and ten. I had just started a new job with a large publishing company, and life was good.

Then the page turned. A mole on my breast with a lump underneath was nagging me. I had shown it to my gynecologist the previous year, but he said it was nothing to worry about. During my next yearly exam (in September 1984), I mentioned the lump had grown. He still thought it was nothing to worry about, but told me I could ask a surgeon to remove it if I was concerned. Being a bit of a worrier at that time in my life, I saw the surgeon and had a biopsy. He could not get the whole lump out while I was awake, and he said there was a piece left about the size of a pencil eraser. The lump that was "nothing to worry about" turned out to be malignant, and surgery was scheduled for the next week to remove it.

Since the lump was fairly high up on my breast a plastic surgeon had done my biopsy. He wanted to be in the operating room to close my incision. While I was still on the table, the oncology surgeon who performed the lumpectomy asked him to locate the leftover pencil-eraser sized piece. He

29

couldn't find it. It was completely gone! We know this was a miracle that God had worked in my body.

I woke up from surgery the next afternoon feeling my chest. I was delighted to learn my breast was still with me. A lumpectomy was enough to remove the cancer, followed by seven weeks of radiation. My cancer turned out to be the slowest-growing kind. Fortunately it had not yet spread to my lymph nodes.

 ## *How I Got Through It*

My husband and I were in shock when we received the news. We believed in prayer, but we didn't know how to pray. The church rallied around and prayed for us that Sunday, with support and encouraging words. The night before surgery, our friends gathered together. Laughter filled the room and occupied our minds with something other than fear.

I will always be thankful to God for what He did for me, and for the people who walked alongside me during a fearful time. One couple came over every evening during the last few weeks of my radiation treatments to make dinner and help the boys into bed. I am grateful God never left me alone for a moment. I remain to this day humbled that God chose to let me live. I have lived to see my boys grow up, get married, and grant me with seven beautiful grandchildren. I thank God daily for the miracle of life.

 ## *Action Items*

Hearing that you have breast cancer turns your world upside down. Everyone's story is different. I know now that my situation was far easier than many. I didn't have to go through chemotherapy. I had a supportive husband. I had friends and a church that rallied around me. No matter how challenging your circumstances, God is present. Focus on Him and the eternal hope He provides. Take a moment to write a prayer in the Yearbook page that follows, acknowledging His presence in your life.

❦ *Yearbook*

It Does Get Better

Janet Cable

"Be strong and courageous. Do not be afraid or terrified...
for the LORD your God goes with you; he will never
leave you nor forsake you." ~Deuteronomy 31:6

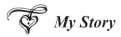 *My Story*

I'm cold, so cold, shivering. I'm sitting in the doctor's waiting room praying that the tiny, suspicious spot on my mammogram was nothing but a shadow. I'm terrified, alone, and so nervous. I'm afraid I'll pass out or throw up.

Two weeks later I'm starting to feel better. *"No news is good news,"* right? But my husband knows what a worrier I am, so while I was at work he called the doctor's office to get an official all clear. Instead the doctor bluntly replied to my husband's inquiry – Oh yeah, she has cancer.

My husband was the one who told me I had breast cancer. This seemed different from how other women had experienced it, or what I had seen in the movies. Before he came to see me he called one of our dear friends, who had breast cancer ten years ago. "I don't know what to do," he asked, "What should I do? How do I tell her?" Our friend advised him to shoot it to her straight, so that's what he did. I was at work when he came and informed me I had breast cancer.

During the first month I felt like I had a dark cloud over my head. "Cancer…*I have cancer,*" I kept mumbling to myself. It was always on my mind. I couldn't shake it. Finally I decided I had enough, and I talked with the Lord. I prayed, "Okay Lord. I can't live like this. We're all going to die sometime so I'm not going to worry any more. I'm giving control back to you, and I will let it go." You see this is not just about cancer. It is about life in general. No matter what happens, I said I would give Him control. After that, the cloud went away.

 ## How I Got Through It

Helping others proved to be helpful in letting go of the cloud. I attended a cancer support group at my church, and when the leaders moved away they asked me to lead the group. I continue to do it, as a survivor. We have fun in the group and try to forget about our cancer concerns, even if it is just for an hour or so. We pray for each other and hear updates on how everyone is doing. God has answered our prayers as we have seen some healing take place. We share our experiences and talk freely with one another. I remembered the Bible verse from Deuteronomy 31:6 when I went in for radiation, and shared with the group how it brought me strength. I focused on the word "hope," and I trusted that God would help me to get through this. Helping others and attending the support group has helped me in my own healing process.

 ## Action Items

Some ladies find it difficult to join a support group until after they have finished treatment. Initially I didn't want people to know that I had cancer, so I didn't want to go to a support group. I didn't want to be singled out because something was wrong with me. I wanted people to accept me as I had always been, and not as one with cancer. Others go right after they are diagnosed. It is a personal choice; give yourself permission to do what is best for you.

For this Action Item it can be helpful to make a list of support groups in your area so you can attend one when you are ready. You might ask your oncologist or social worker to guide you. Contact some local churches or cancer clinics in your area, or you might join an online support group. Reflect on this idea in the Yearbook page that follows.

Yearbook

Support With Love

Sonia Ostrander

*"I can do all this through him who gives
me strength." ~Philippians 4:13*

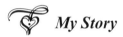 **My Story**

I had a lump in my throat because I had a lump in my breast! Both my mother and grandmother had ovarian cancer, but did not survive. Now I had breast cancer. Would I die too? I was consumed with fear.

When I called my daughter to let her know about the cancer diagnosis she said, "I will be there." My daughter worked for Susan G. Komen˚ in Colorado and was very knowledgeable about breast cancer. She immediately took over my care and treatment. She made many trips from her home in Denver to Houston where I was living, making sure that I was receiving the best treatment.

The first lumpectomy resulted in margins that were not clear so I went in for a second surgery. This time the margins were clear. Surgery was followed with six weeks of daily radiation, to which my pacemaker objected. Twice I had to have the pacemaker reset due to the radiation treatments. It was a first for the technicians who treated me! Thankfully, my cancer did not require chemotherapy.

As a parent we expect to support, help and encourage our children through life, not the other way around. I was so grateful to have my daughter walk alongside me during my treatments. Cancer taught me that I can and need to accept support, help and encouragement from others. It does make a difference.

 ## *How I Got Through It*

At the time I was diagnosed and throughout treatment, I was working at an elementary school. It was hard to be down, sad or worried with students giving me hugs and saying, "Ms. O, I love you." The teachers and all the school staff would check on me and offer me hugs. Precious students made me cards and even decorated luminaries for me that were displayed at the local Relay for Life event.

 ## *Action Items*

Accept the help of others. Your family, friends, co-workers and neighbors want to help—let them. Reach out to others who have experienced breast cancer. Join a support group. You are not alone. Journal your thoughts in the Yearbook that follows. Allow your feelings to flow freely as you capture them with words.

Yearbook

Camp Song

Vicky Conover

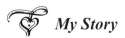 *My Story*

My breast cancer was triple negative and I had seven positive nodes. Because of this my oncologist indicated that if it were going to spread, it would most likely spread to another organ within the first year or two. But after the first two years, I would be fine. Unlike the positive breast cancers where you can have a cell hiding for 20 or more years, I would know within 1-2 years whether it would spread.

Walking to my car, I was mad about the information I had received from my doctor. My husband told me to turn on the radio. I pushed the button, and the radio played a song by Jeremy Camp titled *Walk by Faith*. In that instant God gave me peace. Ten years later, I still react emotionally whenever I hear this song. Admittedly, I still feel a certain level of concern, but He has blessed me with an immense peace. I am still walking by faith. I fall asleep at night, and I sleep peacefully. With that, I am so grateful.

 *How I Got Through It*

I believe the Lord gave me Jeremy Camp's song; it really helped me. Every time I would feel down in the dumps, *that song* would come on the radio, and I knew I could walk by faith. *Walk by Faith* helped me get through the first two years of wondering whether my cancer would spread, and it has stuck with me for the past ten years. This song depicts the importance of walking by faith, regardless of the struggles we face.

> *"Would I believe You when You would say, Your hand will guide my every way? Will I receive the words You say every moment of every day?*
>
> *Well I will walk by faith, even when I cannot see it. Well because this broken road prepares Your will for me.*
>
> *Help me to win my endless fears. You've been so faithful for all my years. With one breath You make me new. Your grace covers all I do."*
>
> *I'm broken, but I still see Your face. Well You've spoken, pouring Your words of grace."*[i]

 Action Items

Listen to Jeremy Camp's song, or read the lyrics above, and reflect on the faith God has instilled in your heart. Having faith doesn't mean we will always hear good news. It does mean we will have someone to walk with us through the storms. When you hear bad news, find a way to alter your day to something more positive, while relying on the faith God gives you. A bad moment doesn't have to turn into a bad day. A bad day doesn't have to turn into a bad week. Commit to reading or listening to something encouraging on a daily basis. Look for inspiration in a sunrise, sunset, a song, another person or situation. Rate your faith in God on a scale of 1-10, and record your thoughts in the Yearbook page that follows. Consider how you might increase your faith by one number as you journal your thoughts.

Yearbook

Not Pretty in Pink

Rachel Livingston

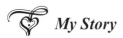 *My Story*

Pink ribbons. Everywhere! I am young and from the social media generation. I have shared my life online for nine years: college graduations, weddings, job promotions, babies, and now, breast cancer. From the day I announced my diagnosis on Facebook, the pink ribbons appeared *everywhere*. People would mail me pink ribbon jewelry, blankets, t-shirts, pillows, bandanas, and more. You name it. I have it festooned with pink. Being young, I am the first of my peers to have breast cancer. And I honestly think they didn't know what to do, or how to help, so they threw pink ribbons at me. And I hated it. Every single pink ribbon, *I hated*. To me it was yet another reminder that I had breast cancer.

I thought my friends were trying to "pretty" my cancer up for me, but I wanted to scream that *nothing* about this is pretty. To me, the pink ribbon was ugly. Then, mid-chemotherapy (mid-hell) came October. You know, "Breast Cancer Awareness *(someone please shoot me)* Month," and the pink vomit overflowed. Every single day people would post about me on Facebook: "This week I'm wearing pink for Rachel" (insert selfie) or they would post more stupid pink ribbons on my Facebook wall. One well-intentioned friend actually wrote, "Happy Breast Cancer Awareness Month!" Happy?! *Happy!?!* Is there something about this horrific experience that I am supposed to be celebrating? But I fake smiled at the screen, "liked" their posts and said thank you.

How I Got Through It

I got through the pink bombardment by taking a step back to appreciate the deeper intentions of my friends. I supposed it was okay to be bitter with the cancer the pink ribbon represented, but I realized I should not be bitter toward my friends. I appreciated I had so many people who cared about me—people who thought about me every day during October, as well as other months. So now I *try* to look at the pink ribbon as a symbol that I am not alone.

Action Items

Have there been any cliché moments in your breast cancer journey that have allowed the bitterness in? How about the classic phrase, "At least you're getting a boob job"? Identify some of these unintentional insensitive moments that left you angry. Look past the anger and try to find the good intentions behind each word or action. And once you do, know that you will someday be truly empathetic towards women who will go through this after us.

Yearbook

Tender I Love You's

Noreta Bish

"But God showed his great love for us by sending Christ to die for us while we were still sinners." ~Romans 5:8 (NLT)

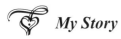 *My Story*

My friend, Debbie, came to visit me several days before surgery and gave me a basket full of wrapped gifts. She said God had impressed on her that the next 30 days were going to be very difficult for me, so she put together a basket of 30 gifts – one to open each day. She said God told her not to number them, that I would open the one I needed each day. I was overwhelmed by her gift. The next day, in my quiet time, I read something that said, "Watch for God's tender I love you in unexpected ways." I realized that Debbie's gift was God's way of reminding me of His love when I so desperately needed to experience it.

 How I Got Through It

I have journaled for years, and it was especially helpful to me as I went through my diagnosis, surgery and recovery. As I look back at those journals, they are loaded with scriptures that supported me, gave me strength, hope, courage and comfort. I was given a book called *Praying Through Cancer*, which was also a tremendous help. I've passed it on to several others as they've gone through their own battle with breast cancer.

The support of my family and church family was tremendous. They planned and provided meals for us for a month after my surgery. My mom and husband took care of me in the weeks after my surgery when I could do little for myself. Our daughters came to the house and washed and styled my hair for me several times a week. They "beautified" me for almost six weeks, until I had use of my arms and could do it myself. God demonstrated His love for me through many supportive people, and for that I am grateful.

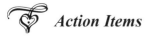 ## Action Items

Watch for God's tender "I love you" in unexpected places. Write about one such experience in the Yearbook page that follows. If you are experiencing writer's block, you might start by finishing this sentence: "God told me He loves me by …" Just let the words flow without self-judgment of grammar or spelling.

Yearbook

One Flesh

Cathy Donaldson

"For in Christ Jesus you are all children of
God through faith." ~Galatians 3:26

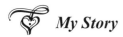 ***My Story***

I was diagnosed with breast cancer in November 2013. The day after diagnosis, I wrote the following letter to our friends and family.

* * *

Not sure where to start and staring at a blank screen, I am tempted to jump into the details of what happened when and what happens next and what we think we know and what questions we need to ask and how we feel. I am smiling now typing this because I know exactly where to start ... not with what or when or how, but with certainty about Who and Whose.

I am *certain* of whose I am ...
I am the *daughter* of the King of Kings, created by Him and for His glory.

I am *certain* of who I am ...
I am Mrs. Ed Donaldson, one flesh with him, bearing cancer in our one flesh.

I am Mom to a handful of kids, and we are about to learn a big lesson together on suffering.

Within a few minutes of the news yesterday, Ed asked me to tell him clearly what I want. My reply was "to be healed of cancer and for God to be glorified in the process". Then, he asked me what I thought God wanted (Gulp). I told him that I thought God wanted to be glorified and that He may heal me in the process. Ed smiled and agreed. And I agree. So that is where we are - keeping our focus on glorifying the One who made us, who suffered for us, and who saved us. And we are going to fight cancer while we are at it!

 ## *How I Got Through It*

Before cancer, I knew the truth of *whose* I was and *who* I was. During the early days of cancer, remembering and re-remembering that truth was the only truly steady anchor I had. Sometimes, in the midst of the shock of diagnosis, I couldn't bring myself to that point or remember myself. Looking to the people who knew me well and loved me best was like a life ring, bringing me back time and time again when the waves of despair crashed around me.

 ## *Action Items*

What is the truth you know for sure? Are you sure you are sure? Who tosses life rings to you? Who can you throw a life ring to this week? Record your thoughts in the Yearbook page that follows.

Yearbook

Unrealized Angel

April Phillips

"He will never leave you nor forsake
you." ~Deuteronomy 31:6

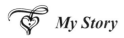 *My Story*

I thought love was supposed to last forever, and then I got breast cancer. I was diagnosed with Stage IV, and they told me the chances of survival were only 14%. But, I had the best doctors in the world; they called me a miracle child.

They saved my life, but the doctors could not save my marriage. With ongoing treatments and changes in my appearance, decreased energy level, inability to think clearly and generally relate, my husband decided he had enough. He distanced himself and eventually we split up. I was still in treatment, and the once cloudless sky grew darker over my head.

Many people support those with cancer, but others just don't know how to act when someone close to them gets ill. They have trouble letting it all be about the patient, as they are struggling and writhing inside with a desperate plea to "notice me! I'm hurting too! My life has just been turned upside down!" They fear death, but even more they fear surviving without their loved one. Or in some cases, they may exploit this circumstance as a "good" excuse to leave. Cancer will test any relationship, and only those swathed by strong purpose and commitment will survive. I am a survivor. I have survived failed relationships, and I am surviving cancer.

How I Got Through It

To be completely honest, when I was asked this question I thought, "I have absolutely no idea how I got through it." However, there is another side to my story. While my husband was unable to support me, I had to let it go. I soon learned that caregiving might come from the place you least expect. It may not even be an adult who supports you the most. Sometimes the greatest prop is a child. This was true for me.

My sister had tried for years to get pregnant unsuccessfully, so when my niece was born in 2010, we were elated. She was two years old by the time I started chemotherapy. In my heart I believe God sent her for me. My fear is not dying; I fear she will grow up and I will not be there to be a part of her life. For that reason, I continue to fight this battle. I do not believe I would have made it if I didn't have my little niece in my life.

She called me "T" because she couldn't pronounce my name. She would come up to me when my hair fell out and my head was shaved and say, "T, you're so fuzzy. Can I touch you?" warming my heart with her innocent smiles. When I was sick from chemotherapy and lying in bed, she would tell those in the room "Shh! T is sleeping." She pushed me when I didn't want to move forward. The doctors saved my body, but this child saved my life.

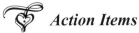 *Action Items*

You have a purpose. You have a reason for being here. Fight! If you don't fight you will never find the reason for living. The journey will be worthless. When you fall, get on your knees and pray. Push yourself and get back up. Ask God to make you aware of someone in your path, whether a little child or an adult, who can walk through this journey with you. He will provide you with a support person if you are open and listen to His voice. If you feel like you have no one, acknowledge God is with you on the journey. People may leave us, and they may disappoint, but the Lord will never fail us. Write about your purpose for living in the Yearbook page that follows.

Yearbook

_____

_____

_____

_____

_____

_____

_____

_____

_____

_____

_____

_____

_____

_____

_____

_____

_____

_____

_____

_____

_____

_____

_____

_____

_____

_____

_____

_____

Fore!

Nana Kay

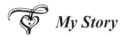 *My Story*

It was the summer of 1984, and I was playing lots of golf. Somebody should have yelled "Fore!" because they were about to hit me with the result of my biopsy. It was malignant. Three lymph nodes were cancerous, and nodes four and five were beginning to become involved. Type? Who knew in the 1980s?

Wow! Sounds like a death sentence!! At the time, I remember reading, "Sixty percent of those with lymph node involvement won't make it."[5] The panic, the unbelievable fear, and the most horrible parts were the hurt and concern that I was causing my family. Why? Because mothers always fix things, put on the Band-Aids, make everything feel better, and assure everyone that it'll be alright. Not this time! How could I live with this?

I felt compelled to talk to my golfing friend Marilyn. She had breast cancer about five years prior to mine and she was still alive. That was very important to hear! Most breast cancer victims at that time weren't so lucky. You never heard about a survivor. Those who survived cancer chose to keep it to themselves. But not this time! They came out of the woodwork to support me and love me and give me encouragement! I decided I was a lucky duck. They didn't send me home to die. They were taking the time to give me chemotherapy. So, I began to be thankful. I made goals for myself to be on the golf course 6-8 weeks after my surgery.

I found myself playing one of my best friends in the finals of a tournament at the country club shortly after I had undergone my reconstruction. I always thought I played best if I looked good, so I had on my brand new Laura Baugh golf outfit: Kelly green shirt, and Kelly, navy and white skirt. It was a humid day and quite sultry, and I sweat easily! After the tournament, a friend asked me what had happened to my shirt. No one had wanted to disturb me while I was playing so well (I won in sudden death). My pretty Kelly green shirt was completely darkened from perspiration, except the spot right over the left (reconstructed) breast, which was dry as could be. My reconstructed breast didn't sweat! What a picture to be shared with all those onlookers!

I hoped the 13-year old male caddie didn't notice, and prayed the Archie Bunkers on the first tee box were too anxious to get on the course to figure that one out! But the victory and the camaraderie of my golfing friends provided giggles that were the beginning of many, as I dealt with only one boob on my journey! All I wanted, I would say, was to be normal again.

 ## *How I Got Through It*

You can probably sense from my story that my sense of humor got me through my cancer diagnosis and treatment, and has helped me in the years that followed. Life's too short to be taken too seriously. I decided to enjoy life and the unexpected fun that creeps up because of my reconstructed breast. At this writing, I am preparing to celebrate my 75th birthday next month and I feel as if I am still 40 or 44 (sans a little energy), the age when I was diagnosed with breast cancer.

 *Action Items*

Take it from me, a long-term breast cancer survivor who fought challenging odds—your diagnosis does not have to be a death sentence! And it doesn't have to stop you from doing the things you love. Find humor in your situation and write about it in the Yearbook page that follows. Set a goal to accomplish one thing you love. Be sure to write it down.

Yearbook

Inward Renewal

Lucinda West

*"Therefore we do not lose heart. Though outwardly
we are wasting away, yet inwardly we are being
renewed day by day. For our light and momentary
troubles are achieving for us an eternal glory that
far outweighs them all." ~2 Corinthians 4:16-17*

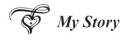 **My Story**

A passage of Scripture received new ink in my Bible one morning while I was undergoing treatment for breast cancer. The Scriptures related to suffering were jumping out at me like never before. Verses I never previously underlined contained new meaning. This is what I love about the Bible. It contains meaning for each person, new situation, and moment. Maybe I have not suffered enough before now, but these stood out to me that particular morning.

Having breast cancer and going through treatment generates a great deal of suffering. Our bodies suffer, our families suffer, our jobs suffer, our housework suffers, and the list goes on and on. I imagine you can relate to this concept.

Of all the many people in the Bible, the Apostle Paul understood suffering. In reality, my suffering is insignificant compared to his. He didn't have pre-medication to help with the side effects of his beatings like we have for our chemotherapy. He didn't have a warm blanket to cover him when he was cold and naked, or trampled with stones. And he didn't have a spinal block to prevent his nerve endings from shouting in pain. My platelets may be dropping, but I am not left for dead! I can go to the hospital, but he was sent to jail. Yet, he still praised God.

2 Corinthians 4:15 may provide a reason for our suffering "all this (Paul's suffering) is for your benefit, so that the grace that is reaching more and more people may cause thanksgiving to overflow to the glory of God." I paused and thought about how many people may benefit from my suffering. I was reminded about the phone calls, emails, and messages I had received from people around the world who were learning and growing because of my story.

How I Got Through It

Verses 16-17 stood tall on the page, and helped me get through my times of suffering. This Scripture written by the Apostle Paul helped me the most through my entire journey. In fact, this one I memorized and wrote down on a card to reference on a daily basis. Here's how I broke it down.

"Therefore, we do not lose heart. Though outwardly we are wasting away." Isn't that the truth? I often felt like my body was wasting away during the treatment process. *"Yet inwardly we are being renewed day by day."* Chemotherapy flows throughout the veins, cleansing my body of cancer, so while I may feel like I am wasting away, there is inward renewal. Yet this is talking about spiritual renewal, which I have also experienced as a result of this journey. Each day has brought me closer to the Lord. *"For our light and momentary troubles are achieving for us an eternal glory that far outweighs them all."* Light and momentary trouble? Wow. That really put my own suffering into perspective. If Paul perceived his suffering as light and momentary, surely I can do the same. Focus not on the present circumstance, but on eternal glory.

 *Action Items*

Do you feel like you are "wasting away?" Don't lose heart. Consider how your suffering may be renewing you inwardly. What strength of character is developing as a result of your suffering? How is this bringing you closer to your family, friends, and God? Focus on the future in the Yearbook page below.

Yearbook

Support

Ivy D. Moore

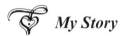 *My Story*

I have been diagnosed with breast cancer twice. The first time it was triple negative in the left breast, and the most recent occurrence in 2013 was ER+ in the right breast. I am a social worker and specialize in women's health. In the hospital where I work, nine or ten nurses were also diagnosed with breast cancer within the last seven years. We all had this one thing in common; it was kind of odd. My oncologist thought it was odd as well.

I've always been independent, and I felt like I should be able to handle this cancer on my own. So, in 2009 when I was diagnosed the first time, I only told a couple of friends. This second time, however, I knew I had to do things differently. The second diagnosis knocked me to my knees. I tried to be strong and positive for the kids, but I needed help. I decided to allow others to step in and help me. I wanted them to know their support altered my day.

People babysat the kids, picked them up from school, and showered my family and me with cards. Over one hundred people expressed love and showed support. It was wonderful!

How I Got Through It

People asked, "How can you go through this?" Support. When you are diagnosed, it's important to reach out—even if it's just to one person. The more support you can get, the better.

 ### *Action Items*

If you lack support, your first step is to find out what services your clinic or hospital offers. Ask the physician or nurse practitioner. Do you have a social worker? Case manager? Make an appointment with this person. They can put you in touch with local agencies that can provide you with the support you need. It's not a sign of weakness. This is a time in your life when you need support, and you should ask for it.

Realize that there will be bad days, and it's okay to have a bad day. Try to be strong enough not to let that bad day turn into a bad week. Give yourself permission to have a bad day. You've been dealt this really big blow. Now visualize tomorrow, getting out of bed, and doing one thing around the house. Go get the newspaper or check the mail. Something simple. It may seem insignificant, but that's okay. You don't have to climb Mount Everest. Just do something to make tomorrow a better day. Write down some things you might do if you have a bad day. Turn it into a better day.

Yearbook

The Drive Home

Christine Potter

"For nothing is impossible with God." ~Luke 1:37 (NLT)

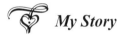 *My Story*

My surgeon named me "The One In A Million." Each time he went over what procedures they would be doing along with the risk factors, he would say, "I need to tell you about this, but it's like a one in a million chance it will happen." Yep, it would happen to me; but at least I haven't died from all the surgeries.

One day while driving home I was thanking God that I didn't have another chemotherapy treatment that week and it was the weekend. Work had been taking a toll on me as well. All I needed to do was get home, relax, and try not to do anything all weekend.

I wished the air conditioner worked better in this car but I was thankful that I even had a car and no car payments. Having such long hair during a Florida summer was not helping matters either. There's a hair tie on the shifter. I'll just pull it up and get it off my neck.

What? Just what I had been waiting for; looking down at my hands I noticed they were covered with hair. *How am I going to explain this to a 4 and 6 year-old?* By the time I got home the floorboard of my car had collected a pile of brown hair.

Here goes nothing. The girls were running out the door to greet me.

After all the greetings and looking over their artwork from daycare, we sat down to talk. "Girls, remember how mommy goes to the doctors on some Fridays and gets a special medicine to get rid of the cancer?" I remember smiling as their little blonde heads were bobbing up and down. "And we said that my hair would be falling out one day because of the medicine, but would grow back after I was done taking the medicine?" Heads were still bobbing up and down. "Let me show you something neat I can do." I ran my hands through my hair and showed them how it came out.

They asked if it hurt. "No, not at all. Would you like to try and see how easy it comes out?"

"YES!!!" I didn't expect that kind of excitement. Their heads kept bobbing. "Wow, that's cool mom. Can I do it again?"

We would be out and the girls would say, "Watch what my mom can do," And they would pull a handful of hair out, laughing and saying "isn't that cool?"

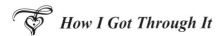 ## *How I Got Through It*

This was the moment that I decided not to let my imagination run away with crazy ideas and the "what ifs." I determined I could only control the moment I am in, with the help of prayer, faith, patience and a loving family. Faith: it does not make things easy—it makes them possible.

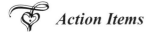 ## *Action Items*

Don't be afraid to share your journey with your children at their level. How might you use humor and your imagination (and a little faith) to make it through each treatment day? Jot down your thoughts about this in the Yearbook page that follows.

Yearbook

My Big Girl Façade

Cindy Moore

"Search me, God, and know my heart; test me and
know my anxious thoughts." ~Psalm 139:23

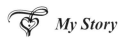 **My Story**

The beast was 5.5 centimeters and had been removed by the surgeon. I cried and became angry, then put on my big girl façade and decided to fight. Later, when the sentinel node biopsy was performed at the same time the chemotherapy port was implanted, I cried again. I then wiped my tears with a warm cloth provided by an understanding recovery nurse, put on my big girl façade, and remarked that it was time to get on with this fight.

Many times I was able to put on the big girl façade. There were other times when I would stretch out on the floor and just talk to God. I would ask Him to make me better, help me not to be a burden to others, and to help me to breathe—sometimes it was hard to even do that. And I whined—a little girl in trouble whine.

Husband, friends, co-workers, along with brothers and sisters in Christ—oh, how they helped. They went to chemotherapy with me, took me to office visits after the mastectomy, made me hats, let me talk when I wanted to, and left me alone when I didn't. One loving, levelheaded co-worker told me to calm down after a steroid induced fit about nothing in particular. I love her to this day.

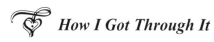

How I Got Through It

A brother in Christ once asked me to explain suffering to the Wednesday night church crowd, and none of the typical thoughts—the treatments, puffiness, inability to breathe at times, the neuropathy and foot pain—none of that came to my mind. The only thought I could muster was that suffering is separation from God, and because Christ saved me, I didn't have to suffer. Was that a little bit of false bravado? I am not a super-Christian so I wondered if I would stand up to the test if circumstances were different and I was bed-ridden or had another malady of some kind.

Many times, as various trials came my way, it crossed my mind that God let me know back on that Wednesday night that I would have more physical and spiritual tests and that He would be with me each and every time. All I had to do was call on Him. You see, there is a tiny little girl in me that God Himself created. He let me whine and put on the big girl façade whenever I thought I needed it. But, He has been standing beside me all the while, ready to take over when I finally ran out of my own power and ability to control. That false sense of power and control is the real façade, because God Himself is my strength, my source, and the lover of my life.

There was nothing then—nothing in the present nor anything in the future that my God can't handle in His own way. His hand is the filter, and He is the master of my life.

Action Items

I am learning to bend my knees at the moment God lays something on my heart, mostly when I again think the big girl façade is enough to get me through. Have you ever tried to use the big girl façade? How did that work for you? Or have you turned over your suffering to allow God to be the source of strength? Reflect on this in the Yearbook page provided.

Yearbook

A Curse or a Blessing?

Sonia Clayton

"It is always darkest just before the
Day dawneth." ~Thomas Fuller

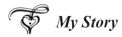 *My Story*

When I saw my doctor to discuss my cancer diagnosis, he was shocked to see how calm I was to learn this terrifying news. I didn't cry. I didn't ask why. I didn't ask how it happened. I didn't even care. It was as if I was expecting the culprit and was looking forward to an end to my life.

Cancer is a big journey, a huge challenge, and a major undertaking. The moment you enter the "valley of the shadow of death" (Psalm 23) with the news of cancer, things rapidly change. You quickly discover that life is a gift from God. Life is something wonderful. You also learn that a life of belief teems with thrills, boldness, danger, shocks, reversals, triumphs, and epiphanies. And you want to fight hard for the gift of life.

Traveling on the dusty trail, crossing mountain peaks and wandering through valleys with breast cancer, however, changed my perspective on life. I learned to embrace life. I accepted Christ's love. I asked my doctor to pray with me before my surgery. He held my hand tight and closed his eyes. I then said my prayer in a loud voice. By this time I had gained some renewed appreciation for life and I had a special request from God. It was a request "for life." I asked Him to guide the hands of my surgeon so he could operate with "divine precision" and remove my cancer. Surgery was indeed a success!

I found the love of Christ and the miracles of His blessings in the anguish and distress of cancer. It is "always darkest before the Day dawneth," as the old saying goes. Often an individual reaches that dark point during the phase preceding His ultimate victory.

 ## How I Got Through It

For some people cancer is a curse, but for me it has been a gift and a blessing. It was through my breast cancer journey that I learned to value the gift of life. With determination, I worked every day after my surgery and during my radiation treatment. It was at that point where I understood that God was very aware of who I was. He was in control and putting order in my soul. My spirit was lifted and I felt the joy of life again.

God answered my prayers, for my children as well as my health. He made Himself very apparent to me. I felt as if God wanted me to know that He was there for me, although I previously didn't think He was. At times, I could hear the whisper of His voice telling me that He was very much in charge and that He was going to take care of my problems one by one.

 ## Action Items

First and foremost, I congratulate you, my cancer sister, on your strength and courage while going through this season of your life. There is nothing easy about cancer, but fighting hard for our lives is doable. We are definitely marked women with energy diminished into fatigue by the fight. Regardless of your circumstance, remember that you were given this life because you are strong enough to live it!

List three reasons to continue living. Put these on a note card and carry them with you. Bring out the card whenever you are tempted to give up or feel sorry for yourself. In the Yearbook page that follows, write a prayer and accept God's unconditional love.

Yearbook

Laughter is the Best Medicine

Tanya McKelvey

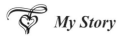 *My Story*

My overall treatment plan was in this order: chemotherapy, healing, single mastectomy, healing, 30 daily radiation treatments, healing, followed by breast reconstruction. Looking back on all these phases, things seem like one big blur. The trauma of it all fades away while various memories and life lessons evolve.

A significant day for me happened half way through my radiation. I was in what I came to think of as my pin-up girl pose for radiation; one hand was behind my head and one was on my hip. The technologist was preparing me and the machine for my treatment and as always music was playing in the background. The songs that day I'd describe as a Dean Martin-like style; and this one song came on that contained a wolf whistle! There I was, with one breast cut off, posing, and someone was giving me a wolf whistle!

I was by myself, and started to laugh so hard I cried. I was a mess when the female technologist came back in, and asked me what was wrong. I told her, and we had a good laugh together. Of course male techs helped me on other days, but this particular day I was sure glad it was a lady tech who could understand my emotions!

How I Got Through It

I had an appointment right after radiation that day with my radiation oncologist. I reviewed the day in radiation treatment with her. And while it may not have been an original saying, she insightfully remarked while laughing too, "Yes, laughter can be the best medicine."

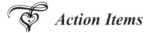

Action Items

Keep looking for the light side, or humor, as you work through your treatment plan. It helps you stay sane! Record thoughts of humorous things you have encountered in the Yearbook page that follows. If you can't think of something humorous, look at the comics in the newspaper and have a laugh or two.

Yearbook

Keep on Running

Beverly J. Points

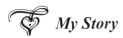 *My Story*

My breast cancer journey was truly more of an inconvenience than a tragedy. I attribute it completely to God answering lots of prayers by dear friends at church, my family and friends I've met online.

The worst time I experienced was during the second phase of chemotherapy. I had a couple of bad weeks with all kinds of gastrointestinal problems. I remember feeling miserable and wondering how I'd ever make it through another month of chemotherapy.

In church that week, one of the young pastors who had been a track coach before going into the ministry preached a profound message. As a part of the sermon, he showed a video clip of a women's track meet. In it, one of the runners tripped and fell flat on her face, yet she got back up and ended up winning the race. What a message for me! It helped me to realize that even though I'd pretty much fallen down at that point, I could – and would, with God's help – still win the breast cancer race!

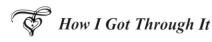

How I Got Through It

A dear friend gave me the book *The Red Sea Rules* by John Morgan[6] while I was waiting for my diagnosis. One of the principles in the book challenged me with, rather than whining "why me?" I should focus on "how can God be glorified?" It made all the difference! I memorized and repeated a mantra, a quote by Andrew Murray, over and over throughout my treatment (for example, the day when I had an MRI, ultrasound, Pet scan and echocardiogram all in the same day, I said it about 100 times). The mantra is this: "I am here by God's appointment, in His keeping, under His training, and for His time."

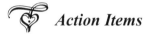

Action Items

When you feel like you are falling, look to the end of the race. Get up and keep on running. If you can't run, walk! Think of similarities between running a marathon and the race to beat this disease. Focus on the goal of finishing the race as you write your thoughts in the Yearbook page that follows. Think about what you would like to be doing a few years from now, after breast cancer.

Yearbook

Just Like Mommy

Cathy Donaldson

But the wisdom from above is first pure, then peaceable,
gentle, open to reason, full of mercy and good fruits,
impartial and sincere. ~ James 3:17 (ESV)

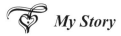 *My Story*

Early in my cancer treatment, we took a field trip downtown Houston to MD Anderson Cancer Center. Oh, how exciting! I know. Here is the story of that day.

When I got up this morning, the whole day stretched before me and I thought about all the things I could get done. And then I got a little overwhelmed, so I started thinking through the list of things only I can do. Still overwhelmed. So then I thought about what things I might not feel up to doing soon. And then, finally, I thought about what the kids *really* needed from me today.

If I were an eight-year-old boy or a seven-year-old girl or a five-year-old boy, and I knew my mom had cancer, I would want to know more about what she was doing to get better. I would want to see that place. I would want to meet those people.

So that's what we did today. We drove to the Medical Center and parked in the garage, just like Mommy does. We went to the Breast Center and sat in the waiting room, just like Mommy does. We walked around and looked at artwork and sculptures, just like Mommy does. We rode the golf cart through the big blue tube, just like Mommy does. We had a snack in the cafeteria, just like Mommy does. And we rode home tired, just like Mommy does.

It was a good day, mostly. It was hard seeing our kids in that place, knowing they were there because of me.

 ## *How I Got Through It*

As we entered the parking garage to go home, our five-year-old was holding my hand. When the elevator opened and he saw the garage ahead, he stopped suddenly.

"Are we going home?" he asked, confused.

"Yes son," I replied.

"But Mom, we can't go yet. Mom, they didn't cut the cancer off you today."

Wide-open eyes stared at me, baffled. Deep breath in, but tears came anyway. Mine, not his. Then I gave him the best explanation I thought a 5-year-old could carry, and it was as gentle and sincere and I could muster. And that was enough.

 ## *Action Items*

How do you anticipate the needs of the people nearest you? Consider how you will explain your journey with your children or other family members. Your decision about what to tell them, or not tell them, is yours and yours alone. Every woman's journey is different. Write a prayer for your family members in the Yearbook page below.

Yearbook

_____
_____
_____
_____
_____
_____
_____
_____
_____
_____
_____
_____
_____
_____
_____
_____
_____
_____
_____
_____
_____
_____
_____
_____
_____
_____
_____
_____
_____

This is Temporary

Joy Cabanilla

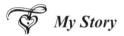 *My Story*

The reality of my journey hit me when I pulled my ponytail holder off and a clump of hair came off with it. I was so upset, I cried. I had long hair then. I couldn't imagine losing it all. But rather than remain sad, I decided to *own it* and shave my head. I didn't want to cut it shorter like some women who like to keep their hair as long as they can. It was more traumatic for me to see bits of my hair fall out. So I got it shaved. I realized my hair would grow back. This was *temporary*.

I was treated initially with the more challenging chemotherapy, nicknamed "red devil." This was later followed by weekly "soft chemotherapy," as we say, for the last three months. I did not have higher risk factors that required adjuvant postoperative radiation so my reconstruction was immediate. I felt blessed about that! The surgeon filled my expanders for three months. Then I finally had the reconstruction done later in the year. It is, well, let's just say "different." But I am alive. This journey hasn't been as rough as I know some others have experienced.

After my bilateral mastectomy, I tried to prepare myself to see the scars post operatively. I took a deep breath and took off the bandages. As I looked in the mirror, my heart stopped. I saw the stitches where my nipples used to be, and I saw the four drainage tubes. Two tubes hung from each side as blood filled each of the bulbs. All I could do was stand and stare at them. I thought, "I looked like something from the Sci-Fi channel."

After the shock of the sight wore off, I began to cry. I cried hard for fifteen minutes but it seemed a lot longer. I realized my body would never be the same again. It was so traumatic for me. Once I cried all the tears I could shed, I looked at myself in the mirror and told myself with a determined voice, "This is *temporary. This too, shall pass. This is not the finished product.*" It was important for me to uplift me.

How I Got Through It

I determined to have a positive attitude! I listened to supernatural healing scriptures that I had on my phone. I listened to them every night and still do! I also listened to them when I was doing the infusions. As much as others say they will be there for you (and they will be there for you), they will never understand how you feel unless they have been in your shoes. Some people will be more supportive than others, and I learned to discern whom I could count on as my means of support.

Action Items

Stay positive! That is half your battle. Stay away from negativity – people and drama. Remember, it's not about them. This is about you and your health. If they don't understand that, maybe it's time to cut the ties. This may be a temporary detachment as you find other people to support you during this challenging journey. Connect with ladies who have been in your shoes and are now doing well. Join a cancer support group. I have met a lot of wonderful folks through my support group who are doing well and have encouraged me through the journey. List the names of some positive people in your life in the Yearbook page that follows.

Yearbook

Shave and a Haircut

Lucinda West

"For we are God's masterpiece. He has created us
anew in Christ Jesus, so we can do the good things he
has planned for us long ago." ~Ephesians 2:10 (NLT)

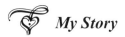 ***My Story***

From my wig stylist's demeanor and expertise, it was obvious she has done this many times before. She described their commitment to maintaining dignity and providing comfort during the process. She was very professional and alleviated my anxiety. She wanted it to be a positive experience, and it was.

Honestly, I viewed this as an opportunity to see something I've never seen before—my head! My back was to the mirror while the clippers buzzed away. When finished she asked, "Do you want me to put on your wig, or would you like to turn around and look at yourself in the mirror first?"

Of course, I wanted to see! "Turn me around!" I admit it was a little shocking at first. I knew I would see a bald head, but I didn't quite know what it would look like on me. I mean, I've lived nearly half a century and I've never seen my own head. That's a little mind-boggling. She said I have the "perfect shaped head," and it was a "pretty head." She probably says that to everyone, but nevertheless, I was impressed.

One thing I hadn't really considered (even though she told me the last time I was in) is that hair keeps your head warm. My head immediately felt the cool of the air, which I believe dropped about 5-10 degrees in temperature. I took her up on the offer to try on some beanies and purchased a royal blue one for sleeping. I was looking forward to enjoying my frizz-free head!

 ### *How I Got Through It*

My family was very encouraging through the whole process. My husband's broad shoulders were evidence of his strength as he supported us all. I couldn't imagine going through this crisis without him by my side. My kids (21 and 15 at the time) also cultivated positivity. A sticky noted with "smile, today's going to be a great day (smiley)" made its way to my bathroom mirror, and the "energy hugs" I got from my daughter kept me going.

Some women wait until their hair falls out completely before having it shaved, while other women never shave their heads. This is a personal choice, and each woman should decide for herself. However, I decided that I couldn't control the loss of my hair, nor could I control my own fate, but I could control my attitude toward it. I didn't want this to become a stumbling block in my journey. I looked forward to seeing my bald head and embraced this temporary "normal" rather than dreading it or running from it.

The verse in Ephesians quoted above has helped me maintain a positive mental attitude. It reminds us, we are masterpieces created by God, to do good things according to His plan. It doesn't matter whether we have hair, good hair, stylish hair, or no hair. He loves us. Period.

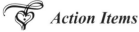 ### *Action Items*

If you are preparing for hair loss, consider purchasing a nice hat or beanie that you can wear when it gets cold. Remember you are God's masterpiece, and He has a plan for your life regardless of whether you have hair or wear a hat or a wig. Spend a few minutes in prayer asking God to share His plan with you (this may take multiple prayer sessions before you hear an answer). Write in the Yearbook page about one "good thing" you would like to accomplish.

Yearbook

The "New Normal"

Cherie Diehl

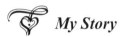 *My Story*

I was lost, confused, and almost out of gas. My third week back to work, my boss asked me to attend a meeting on the other side of town from my home. I will never forget that day. I left my house in plenty of time with directions on my phone. An hour later, I realized the meeting had already started, and I was in a gas station crying—crying because I was disoriented, felt insecure, and realized I had never been this lost, ever!! It took me several minutes to pull myself together and call my husband for help. I completely missed the meeting and my husband had to guide me back home.

This was such a stark contrast to life before breast cancer. Traveling had never been an issue. I had been with this company for 20 years, worked my way up to a position with the division that required travel to multiple stores. People came to me for help and advice. I was the "go-to" person at my job. My mastectomy, chemotherapy, and subsequent hysterectomy disabled me from working for three months, so by the time I went back, I was struggling with self-esteem, energy, different skin, hair loss, hair re-growth, and clothes that no longer fit. I wrestled with my new body and "chemo brain," and wondered what changed while I was gone—what things I had forgotten.

Returning to work brought interesting challenges, like losing my sense of direction, my mind going blank in front of team members, and unexpected

92

conversations with employees who did not know my story. At this point, I was trying my best to return things to normal while working on my energy level, job assignments and getting used to working after three months of being off. Eventually I started feeling normal again.

 ## *How I Got Through It*

I have adjusted well to my "new normal." I am amazed that after only five weeks back on the job I am beginning to feel normal again. The fog has lifted and I no longer feel lost or out-of-place. I meet people every day that probably would never guess that I had breast cancer, so I don't fault those who question my appearance.

I realize the people around me also have a need to understand my changes (physical and emotional). As I seek to understand them, I am less conscientious of my own situation. I kept telling myself that I don't have to share my story with everyone. However, I do need to be understanding of them and their life circumstances. God puts people in our lives at the right moment for a reason, and sometimes that reason is for their benefit. I look for ways to benefit them with my life, and this helps me get through it.

 ## *Action Items*

Welcome to your "new normal." Give yourself time, and understand things will never be exactly the same after breast cancer. Be willing to accept and embrace the new you. Recognize the incredible growth experience. Understand the strength in finding true friends (past and present), how precious each day truly is, and what we do with the time we have.

When you plan to go back to work, take control in advance of how you will approach your story. Think about whether you will tell or not tell your boss, your co-workers, or others about your journey. Establish some planned responses for those unexpected moments when co-workers question your change in hairstyle or why you were out, so you are less likely to be caught off guard. Write some of these thoughts in the Yearbook page that follows.

Yearbook

It's Not About The Hair

Tanya McKelvey

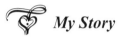 *My Story*

The day I was diagnosed with breast cancer, I went to St. Luke's Hospital in The Woodlands, Texas to do some volunteer work. As soon as my friend heard about my diagnosis, she took me to see the hospital chaplain. He prayed with us, and we witnessed an answer to our prayers when I got into the cancer clinic four weeks earlier than I had previously been told to expect. Father Trego knew I was going to go through chemotherapy and would lose my hair. The next week he gave me a copy of an article, and it stuck with me. It was a transcript of an NPR newscast. I lost my hair twelve days after I started chemotherapy.

 How I Got Through It

Thinking about this article helped me keep things in perspective, and it helped me deal with other people's well-intended but misdirected reactions. It's not about your hair...

> ROBERT SIEGEL, host:
> Commentator Debra Jarvis knows more about cancer than most people. She has been a hospital chaplain for 20 years, and right now she's on the staff of the Seattle Cancer Care Alliance. Last year she herself was diagnosed with breast

cancer and she learned something about cancer that she never knew before.

DEBRA JARVIS reporting:
It's not about the hair, but that's one of the first things people ask me about when I told them I had breast cancer. Will you lose your hair? Some people just assumed I would. There goes the hair, one of my friends said trying to be light and funny. I looked at her and thought, you have terrible hair. You'd love for me to lose mine.

Having cancer was not bringing out the best in me. But the thing is, it's really not about the hair, it's really about death. People die from cancer all the time, but it's so impolite to say, will you lose your life? Much easier to ask about the hair, because if you don't lose your hair, you can almost pretend that you don't have cancer.

Sure, you may be tired and nauseated, your surgery site may hurt, you may have sores in your mouth, your fingernails may be falling off and getting infected, but these are not things that people notice immediately or at all. No one can look at you and say chemo patient.

But if you go bald, you are marked. You can't pretend that everything is normal and that you don't think about death. It's hard for others to pretend that they don't think about death when they look at you. Your bald head shows death in their faces, and most people really hate thinking about dying. So they struggle to ask the right questions. Is asking what's your prognosis too nosey? The answer to that could just lead to more awkwardness. It's safer to ask will your hair grow back?

But here's the good thing about losing your hair, you can't pretend that everything is normal.

One woman who had just lost her hair to chemo said to me, I had chemo for three years and never lost my hair. My family acted as if nothing were wrong. Where are my jeans? Did you call the travel agent? What's for dinner? But now, my God, they're freaking out and falling over themselves to help me.

I didn't lose much of my hair and I worked throughout my treatment. I could pretend that everything was normal, except that every Thursday afternoon, I climbed into a bed, received my chemo and spent the weekend recovering. Someone called my therapy Barbie chemo because I didn't lose all my hair. I would've been furious but I didn't have the energy.

No, it's not about the hair, but people want to make it about the hair because it's so hard to listen to someone talk about fear and pain and grief. But if you can listen to someone talk about those feelings, then when you do talk about the hair, it will really be about the hair. [7]

 ## *Action Items*

As you read this article, consider how you might respond to well-meaning friends who ask about your hair. Will you talk with them on a deeper level, or just keep it light and fun? It's totally up to you how you will respond, and each person may respond differently. Ponder these thoughts as you write in the Yearbook page that follows.

Yearbook

transFORMed

Cathy Donaldson

*"I appeal to you therefore, brothers, by the mercies
of God, to present your bodies as a living sacrifice,
holy and acceptable to God, which is your spiritual
worship. Do not be conformed to this world, but be
transformed by the renewal of your mind, that by testing
you may discern what is the will of God, what is good
and acceptable and perfect." ~Romans 12:1-2 (ESV)*

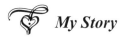 *My Story*

I participated in a LiveStrong program at our local YMCA. The objective
of the program is to improve the physical condition (strength, balance,
endurance) of adult cancer survivors and ultimately get them on
track for lifelong healthy living. The program included everything from
nutrition seminars to an introduction to a variety of different types of
exercise with just the right amount of coaching and encouragement—and
prodding when necessary.

The time is filled with jokes, kindhearted teasing in class, advice and tips
along with fervent prayer in a busy hallway. The instructors have a heart
a mile wide for this—two miles actually. Those women have brought out
my best, time after time. Watching. Helping. Smiling. Pushing. Listening.
And they gave me a precious treasure they didn't intend.

Near the end of the twelve weeks, we had to fill out a form—an evaluation of sorts. For a million dollars, I couldn't tell you what the form asked, except for one question—the one question that has sounded in my head like a gong this past week. *What will prevent you from exercising in the future?* My written response: Death.

Okay, so admittedly, my answer was truthful, but with a dash of snark and a pinch of glib. I meant what I wrote, but frankly, I was ho-hum about the whole form-filling-out thing and when the class session was over, I went on with my day, not giving the form another thought. But then our baby got very sick and was suddenly a hematology patient at Texas Children's Hospital. Day 1—workout was planned but canceled. Day 2—too busy being hideous to my husband (because of stress) to get to the gym. Day 3—still too busy being hideous to my husband to even care about not getting to the gym. Day 4—Texas Children's Hospital, and an epiphany.

 ## How I Got Through It

On the drive home from Texas Children's with our son, I had plenty of time to think. And like a drizzly-February-in-Ohio gust that yanks your umbrella from concave to convex, memories of that LiveStrong form came blowing into all the self-centered, pity-partying recesses of my mind. The memories said *"Death. Death?! Death is what you wrote on the form. Where is that girl now? Nobody has died, especially not you. So what's with all the arguing and excuses?"* Needless to say, I was back in the gym on Day 5.

It might seem a smidge melodramatic to say that one question on one form changed my life. But it did. I wrote the truth on that form, and the truth was compelling enough to cut through all the excuses and do what needed to be done no matter how I felt about it. The form transformed me. Body presented. Tested. Mind renewed. To God alone be the glory.

 **Action Items**

Are there any things in your life that you are avoiding? In the Yearbook, list some of the excuses you have given yourself, and then list a countermeasure to attack each potential obstacle.

Yearbook

An Opponent of Fear

Lucinda West

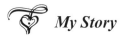 *My Story*

As we lit up the charcoals and roasted hot dogs over the open flame, I realized it had been five days since I was diagnosed with triple positive breast cancer. It was very aggressive and they were going to determine the stage the following day. Our family was traveling in a brand new diesel Ford pick-up at the time, pulling our fifth wheel around the country, and we were still learning to cook over hot coals. We finally had success (third time's a charm) and my husband wished he had a steak to grill after the hot dogs were consumed.

It was a good time for a fun family picnic, for tomorrow would be a full day of testing. I imagined it would not only be a day of testing my physical body, but could also test our emotions and spirituality. It felt like a long day ahead.

We told corny jokes, watched our little dog run her famous circles around the camp, laughed, smiled, and I plunged in the pleasure of my wonderful family. It was a joyful moment as we noticed the stars and watched the coals glow to a bright red, warming our faces as well as our hearts. For a few moments, I "forgot" I had cancer.

How I Got Through It

Each time we prayed before we ate, went to bed at night, and started the day, we asked the Lord to heal my body. My mind went back to the previous Sunday morning. The Pastor's message stuck with me that night by the fire. He spoke about joy being an opponent of fear. When the angel appeared to the shepherds he said, "Do not be afraid. I bring you good news that will cause great joy for all the people" (Luke 2:10). The angel's message was simple: embrace the joy, not fear.

The Pastor anointed and prayed with me at the end of the service. His wife's whisper in my ear at the altar was another reminder not to let cancer rob me of the joy that the Lord had already placed in my heart. This was challenging! While the pressing weight of the next day's consult made it difficult to be joyful, and my human nature tended to be fearful, I decided to stand with James who wrote, "Consider it pure joy, my brothers and sisters, whenever you face trials of many kinds, because you know that the testing of your faith develops perseverance" (James 1:2-3).

Action Items

Are you fearful? Seek joy! Joy requires staying in the present moment. Don't focus on the past or the future. Don't try to control things over which you have no control. Listen to the sounds of nature and look at God's creation around you. Watch the sunrise, or sunset. Smell the dewy air, and as you do this, ground yourself in the present.

Read about the "good news" which the angels proclaimed and look up some quotes on joy. Leave post-it notes around the house reminding you of reasons to be joyful. And make yourself smile! As you record your thoughts in the Yearbook page that follows, consider how you might have joy instead of fear. Write down one or two ways to spread joy to those around you.

Yearbook

Cancer Free

Heather Farris

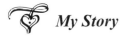 *My Story*

I'll tell anyone who wants to listen to my story. Even if you are young, it can happen to you. You know your body. My doctor said, "You're too young" and was reluctant to do the biopsy. At this point, I didn't know I was pregnant with my third child. I am told that my breasts would have swelled and the cancer would have quickly spread due to being hormone fed from the pregnancy, so I may not be having this conversation if I had not insisted on doing the biopsy. I felt the lump, and I thought I might be going mad. *Maybe it's fibrocystic or caffeine related,* I tried to convince myself. Ten days later, I knew in my heart it was cancer.

The day I was diagnosed, I left work and cried all the way home. All my friends and family descended on my house within an hour. Even my best friend who had just gotten into a car accident came over. "Let's talk through this." They were there to talk it out, support me and just let me cry. I have a strong family and support group. Their presence was all I needed.

I had chemotherapy and surgery while I was pregnant. After my baby was born, I had radiation. I have been cancer free for five years now, and I am stopping Tamoxifen this year. My youngest son is now five years old, and he is healthy. You will get through this!

How I Got Through It

My sisters put together a journey book, from beginning to end. At the end they used the poem "Footprints in The Sand" and inserted my name in there. Jesus was carrying me. I look at the book, and I read it all the time. It is a celebration of life for being cancer-free.

When you are in the midst of treatment, life can become one big blur. It was good to have documentation with pictures and reflections of the different moments in the journey. I don't think I dealt with everything I felt when I was going through treatment. So this was an opportunity to reflect and release.

Action Items

It's okay to cry and have your bad days. As moms, or as women in general, we try to hold it together. I don't think I allowed myself to cry or have many down days throughout the ordeal. When the treatment finally ended, that is when I broke down and cried. This may be the same for you. You may feel the need to stay strong during treatment just to get through it. Then again, you may give yourself permission to have those bad days along the way. Communicate with other women who have been through it and know how you feel. Only another cancer patient or survivor knows your fears, or what's going on in your mind. Other women who have experienced it understand. Record your thoughts in the Yearbook page that follows.

Yearbook

Bitter or Better?

Gail Mills

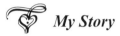 *My Story*

I was on vacation in 2007 with my two daughters and my first granddaughter when I received the call telling me I had breast cancer. We were there visiting my parents to introduce them to their great-granddaughter. I waited until after our family lunch and pondered it a while. My dad was in bad health and I didn't know how this would affect him. How do you tell your dad this is happening? Even so, I'll never forget my mom's response: "You have to beat it."

We flew to a famous cancer research institute for diagnosing and staging. At my first appointment I was scared to death. They ran lots of tests, but one thing that has always stuck with me was the breast MRI. I remember lying in the MRI machine with my face down, tears running down my face the entire time. Then I heard God say, "Everything will be okay. Just relax." At that moment I believed everything would be okay, even if I died.

 *How I Got Through It*

I've always been a Christian, but I actually felt like I met God again in an MRI machine. It was personal. Indescribable. I felt His presence right there with me.

At that moment I decided every time the machine made a different sound, rather than focus on my own destiny I would pray for a different individual in my life. I started praying for my husband, my son, and my parents. My family was well prayed for! From then on, every time I had a treatment I prayed for my family. I spent most of my time in prayer.

I made a choice that day. I thought I had two options. I could be really bitter, or I could learn to be a better person because of this. You either learn something from your experience or you don't.

 ## *Action Items*

When you go down this road, you have two choices: bitter or better. Which will you choose? Write about your choice in the following Yearbook page. If you feel bitter, describe one step you can take toward feeling better. Perhaps today it is difficult to think about feeling better. If this applies to you, give yourself a break. Come back to this page on a regular basis until you begin to overcome the bitterness.

Yearbook

Battle Bikes and Marathons

Lucinda West

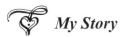 *My Story*

The day before I was to go into surgery to have my mastectomy, I received a notice from a Facebook friend. My name was tagged in a video. Curiously I watched, and what I saw genuinely surprised me.

Alex, a friend of ours from a church we used to pastor, was leaving the next day to ride in the "24-Hours of Booty," an official Livestrong sponsored charity event in Charlotte, North Carolina. Alex explained in his video and shared with many, that he was riding his battle bike in my honor. Many names of cancer victims are placed down the seat tube of the bike, and my name was perched prominently on the crossbar. His video brought tears to my eyes, and touched the hearts of many others as well. I was humbled by his truly heartfelt appreciation for the friendship our family has shared over the years. I was also pleased and honored to learn that riding on the opposite side of the crossbar was the name of a friend, Chris, who was also battling breast cancer for the third time. Chris had inspired me to maintain a positive attitude throughout my journey. We were destined to ride together, and Alex was our champion.

Another time in my journey, Marleta, a friend from Australia, sent me a message on Facebook. She wanted me to know that she and her daughter, Karys, were running in a 5K. They were running this race in my honor, and once again tears of overwhelming appreciation made their way down my cheeks as I reminisced a friendship that spans the globe.

Yet another day while I was enduring daily radiation, I received a package in the mail from my friend Maria. It contained a marathon medal and a note. She had just completed the 2013 New York City Marathon where she had earned a beautiful medal with the city skyline and a pink ribbon embossed on the front. What an accomplishment! Yet, she felt compelled to give her medal to me. Her note stated that I deserved the medal more than she did. She believed my race against breast cancer was more challenging than the one she had just run, and she wanted me to know she was thinking of me the whole time. The medal hangs on the wall beside my desk, where I am constantly reminded of our friendship and a race against breast cancer that has been won.

 ## *How I Got Through It*

Here was my takeaway. None of these individuals did these activities to gain approval or recognition. They were not seeking a reward. They did these acts of kindness because they had a passion to clear this world of a dreaded disease. Often, friends don't know how to help, but in these cases they just did what they do best and I was honored by their kindness.

As I watched the video of the battle bike through blurry, tear-filled eyes, and read the private messages sent by our friends the runners, I recognized the value of friendship. We lived apart, yet they remembered me. I became astutely aware that I was not alone in my journey. Many people were running this race alongside me, encouraging me to put one foot in front of the other when I felt like giving up.

 ## *Action Items*

Who has inspired you? How have others supported you through this journey? Perhaps it is a small act of kindness. Even if you are unaware of it, people are thinking of you. You are not alone. No matter how big or small, reflect on the generosity that has come your way as others reach out to support you. Jot your thoughts down in the Yearbook page below.

🖤 *Yearbook*

Easter Eggs

Cherie Diehl

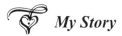 *My Story*

I didn't remember hiding any Easter Eggs in my breast. But that's what it felt like when I ran my hand down my left breast while soaping up in the shower one Easter Sunday morning. I got out of the shower in shock, and showed my husband the exact spot where I felt the lump. *"Does this feel different to you?"* He felt the lump and just told me to call my doctor. That began "our story."

Once my doctor felt the lump, she scheduled a mammogram and ultrasound for the following day. It had been a long time since I had a mammogram. In my mind I beat myself up with negative self-talk about how this was "my fault." Time passes so quickly. *"Had it really been four years since I had a mammogram?"* I lectured myself unnecessarily.

I prayed the night before the tests that God would be with me through this journey. I was convinced I had cancer. My mom was diagnosed in 1986 and she passed away four years later at the age of 40. I was 44 and still alive, at least. I reminded myself that cancer research his come a long way and combated the negativity in preparation for the tests that lied ahead.

The doctor was very friendly. He scanned my breast and told me that I needed a biopsy on two spots, the lump and under the arm (lymph nodes). I was completely in shock. I believed the lump would need a biopsy, but *not the lymph nodes*! I remember smiling as I left the room, smiling as I scheduled my biopsy for the following day, and smiling until I left the building. As I walked outside heading to my car, the smile faded and I wept.

I debated with myself about whom to call. I had already put so much on my husband this week, but I needed to hear from someone that it would be okay. What a relief when I dialed my best friend and I heard her voice. She knew about my appointments and listened to me through my tears as I told her I was having two biopsies—two spots to be checked. As I explained, she listened to my fears, disappointments, and cried with me.

 ## How I Got Through It

Crying has multiple benefits. As my friend cried with me we released toxic chemicals from our bodies. But I am also aware that too much crying can be unhealthy; I knew I couldn't stay there. I believed I had to do something fun as I was ruminating about the upcoming biopsy.

I thought, *"If they have to look at my boobs again, I am going to give them something to look at."* So I drew a happy face on my left breast. Surprise!!! The next day I went back for the biopsy and checked in just like I did with the mammogram. Sitting in the waiting room a nice young lady asked me how long I thought the wait would be. I told her it was okay, and I showed her my happy face. It made us both laugh. The nurse was not impressed with my happy face, but the doctor was! He laughed, so that made me feel better. Now he has a story to tell!

 ## Action Items

When you are being diagnosed, don't search the Internet. Trying to diagnosis yourself just adds to the anticipatory anxiety. If you feel the urge to go online, look up the benefits of crying and journal your thoughts below. Or search for ways to maintain a positive mental attitude in times of crisis. Look for ways to rely on God in these difficult times. If you need to cry, by all means cry! However don't stay there. Also, don't beat yourself up or blame yourself for your cancer. *Remember, it isn't your fault!* Be patient and let God handle it.

Yearbook

Getting Through It All

Frances Schlueter

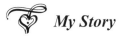 *My Story*

Prolonged illness becomes isolating when healthcare providers become your main source of interaction. My battle stretched out over several years, and the extended fight was exhausting. Setbacks were overwhelming and often I struggled to push forward through ongoing treatments and surgeries. I felt like I existed in a vacuum, moving from my bed to the sofa, resting and trying to recover. My goal was to build up enough energy for the next shoe that seemed certain to drop.

As a two-time breast cancer survivor, numerous complications, infections, and injuries depleted my inner resources and made the journey challenging. It could have been easier at times to give up, but I knew I should keep on fighting. To do so, I had to get creative in finding ways to push through the many obstacles that seemingly blocked the path.

Watching television was my salvation for a while, but I eventually exhausted the supply of reruns and old movies. Cabin fever was constantly peeking around the corner and I needed to change the vibe surrounding me. I love to walk but it was frequently too taxing on my depleted energy level. As a melancholy, monotone beat drummed on my heart, I knew I had to do something different.

The beauty of nature awoke my senses, stirring my attentions from the sofa and television to the swing on my covered porch. I took up residence there and spent many hours swinging and communing with nature. I watched the squirrels and birds, observed life in my neighborhood and became one with the changing seasons. It may seem insignificant, but my time on that swing was meditative and a valued source of rejuvenation.

When my energy improved enough for me to drive, I visited various coffee shops. They were instrumental in connecting me to the outside world, providing an important reminder that I was a part of it. My family and friends all had work and school obligations during the day, so I was typically alone. Rather than sit at home feeling sorry for myself, I would go out, drink fabulous coffee, and document my thoughts and worries into my journal.

Eventually, I felt well enough to be a little more active. My long fight had produced a deep level of physical de-conditioning, and I could barely manage beyond a gentle walk. It felt like I was taking baby steps, learning to walk all over again. But, I put one foot in front of the other.

 ## *How I Got Through It*

My journal has been my source of connecting with myself. It is a place where I can be honest about my journey and struggles. My journals are a treasure to me, as this process helped bring order to the chaos that surrounded my life. Capturing my thoughts in writing seemed to liberate the internal energy I needed to keep fighting my battle. After many years, I can finally say that I feel well! I spent many hours on my porch swing, wondering if I would ever be able to say that.

 ## *Action Items*

What helps bring peace and calmness into your life? What do you do to bring energy to your world? Do you practice these elements on an ongoing basis? What are your most important treasures? As you ponder these questions, write about one source of peace in the Yearbook page that follows.

Yearbook

What We Listen to Matters

Cathy Donaldson

*"Whoever listens to me will live in safety and be
at ease, without fear of harm." ~Proverbs 1:33*

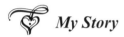 ***My Story***

In my journey through cancer, I have struggled with anger. Dear friends counseled me that anger is frequently a secondary response to a primary instigator. I chewed hard on that and found the gristle. Fear. Fear had taken root in my heart and I hadn't even noticed. I *listened* to the fears whispering at me.

> Fear about money - cancer is a painfully expensive disease.

> Fear about marriage - cancer is corrosive on even the strongest epoxy.

> Fear about mothering - cancer is a wolf eyeing my lambs.

> Fear about homemaking - cancer is a demoralizer extraordinaire.

> Fear about recurrence - cancer doesn't care that *I want to live.*

Fear. Fear. Fear. Fear. Fear. Growing like kudzu, covering and smothering, in the untended garden of my heart.

And then this ...

Whoever listens to Me will dwell secure and will be at ease, without dread of disaster (Proverbs 1:33, ESV).

In the wake of diagnosis and treatment, and bills, and pain, and the air conditioner stopping, and gut-deep sorrow, and the water heater breaking, and the washing machine not washing, and ongoing pain, and kids who need help with math, and the same kids who wanted to eat meals three times per day, I had somewhere started listening to the toothless growls of fear, more than I was listening for the fierce love of my Father.

And that verse ... Proverbs 1:33 ... well, it is captivating to me. *Dwell secure?* Yes, I'd like some of that. *At ease?* Sign me up. Those sound great.

But what about the big one ... *without dread of disaster?* There it is. That's what has been punching me in the gut every day. Dread.

How I Got Through It

If I listen to my Father, I will not have dread of disaster. Not that I won't have disasters. The fact that I even have a page in this book is evidence enough of disaster. Lack of disaster is not the promise. The promise is that I won't dread disaster. The promise is that I will live secure.

I am not so naïve to think that this epiphany will magically fix everything in my heart. I am sure I'll have to weed and re-weed and re-re-weed my garden. But I have learned that what I listen to matters, and that is a place to start.

 *Action Items*

Is there a disaster you dread? Have you named it out loud? Does the *dread* make the disaster any easier? Write about it in the Yearbook page below.

Yearbook

My Journey with Chemotherapy

Marshel Kay Brown Shewmake

"Healing begins when we do something. Healing
begins when we reach out to others. Healing starts
when we take a step forward." ~Anonymous

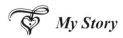 ### *My Story*

My medical oncologist came in with this piece of paper that conveyed the expression, "Beware, danger lies ahead." She acknowledged my breast cancer was stage 2A, but said it was as aggressive as stage 3. I needed six months of chemotherapy or there was fifty percent chance it would come back within ten years and kill me. She must have noticed the potential meltdown, so she assured me six months would go by faster then I thought.

Regardless of her pep talk, I knew chemotherapy would be a long process. Your life is basically put on hold for six months and all you can do is live one day at a time. It was a big blow to my family, and me, but we felt we had little choice in the matter. It takes grit and guts to conquer cancer if you want to live a long life.

 ### *How I Got Through It*

My mother had just gone home to Nebraska after a 6-week stay to help me after surgery, so I didn't want to ask her to come back at this point. Instead,

I turned to God and my church family. Without them, I don't know what would have happened to my husband and me. Having cancer was a hard time for all of us. I asked my Sisters in Christ (the women at my church) for help going to and from chemotherapy. They were all willing to help us. Each week my Sister in Christ would say, "I have made plans to take you to your therapy. What time do I need to be at your house?" Or she would tell me who would be helping me out that week. She organized dependable reinforcements from our caring family at the church, and I did not have to worry about how I was going to get to my treatments every week.

I am so thankful for all their caring and support. It meant a lot to us. Others would send food, cards, call or text me each day to encourage me and let me know they where praying for us. This helped me get through the tough times. I was able to get through my journey with chemotherapy because of their shared commitment.

 **Action Items**

God provided support from my Sisters in Christ. I also know that God was always with my family and me throughout my journey. It was a difficult time, but I survived. If you don't belong to a church family or you have been inactive in your local church, now is a great time to get plugged in! Make an appointment with one of the pastors, and research the services they offer to cancer patients.

At times you will be sick or you may worry when your hair falls out and you have to go out in public looking different than everyone else. You can't do everything on your own. Recognize it is okay to ask for help. The Lord will get you through the hard times and He will always be with you no matter what may come your way. Have faith in Him and you will be victorious. Psalm 37:5 (NCV) says, "Depend on the Lord; trust him, and he will take care of you." Reflect on this Scripture and record your thoughts in the Yearbook page that follows.

Yearbook

Waiting

Lucinda West

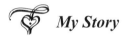 *My Story*

I had heard of cancerous skin that looks like orange peel, but my eyes stared at my breasts through wispy mists in denial of the obvious. Modesty flew out the window as multitudes of people came in the room to examine my uncovered breasts. Due to the skin involvement my diagnosis was uncertain, requiring a team of specialists to decide. Doctors pondered whether it was an aggressive HER2+ breast cancer, or the more serious inflammatory breast cancer (IBC). They openly discussed the possibilities of "treatment" versus "cure."

Later that night, my husband and I did what many cancer patients do. Buried in the quicksand of ignorance, we searched the Internet for answers. According to various websites, IBC is "the worse kind" of breast cancer, with the lowest chance of survival. Despair and doom clouded the bedroom.

Fortunately, we discontinued plummeting into the depths of our own fears as friends provided comfort during the wait. My lifelong friend Jena sent messages of encouragement at midnight, while we were having trouble sleeping. The next day, Dea, another friend whose wife was a cancer survivor, reminded us, *"God is not a God of statistics."* No matter what the Internet says, God is not bound by the Internet's norm. He is in control. The Psalmist affirms: God defies the odds.

While being tested for diagnoses and staging, much to our surprise our friends, Bob and Patty, showed up unexpectedly to wait with us and encourage us. This was quite a sacrifice as they lived four hours away. It was a welcome visit!

How I Got Through It

Overall I'm a pretty patient person. Christmas morning, red lights or long lines do not make me tap my fingers or sigh heavily. I just find other things to occupy my mind as I wait. Waiting for a diagnosis, however, is difficult for even the most tolerant individuals. It was an emotional roller coaster from the moment I heard the "C" word to learning what stage and treatment would be.

If Jena had asked, we might have said, "don't wait up," yet she stayed awake chatting words of encouragement. Or, had Bob and Patty mentioned it, we probably would have said, "That's a long trip. No need to come. We'll be alright." Yet they arrived and stayed in the hospital until we had news. In those moments I realized this is one time in my life when people wanted to help, and it was important to let them. Their presence made the wait bearable. Their presence was vital to our healing and well-being. We would have gotten through it without our friends (I think), but we were so glad we didn't have to!

 Action Items

I recommend you read Psalms 13. King David pours out his heart honestly to God. He is tired of waiting for God to answer. But his mood shifts (verses 5-6) as he trusts in God's unfailing love. Trust in God's love as you wait for your diagnosis or next treatment. I truly believe that God is in control. Find examples of individuals defying the odds when they put their trust in God.

Think about the following questions and journal your thoughts in the Yearbook page: On whom do you rely for support when times get rough? Have you ever brushed off the offer of a friend to help (be honest)? When a friend offers to help, let them! How can you rely on God during the times of waiting? Take a few moments to thank God for His presence in your life, and ask Him to send you a supportive friend.

Yearbook

Pink Christmas

Noreta Bish

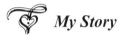 *My Story*

Christmas has always been my favorite time of the year. When I received my breast cancer diagnosis two weeks before Thanksgiving, I knew the holidays would be difficult. Although my cancer was detected early, I tested positive for the BRCA-2 gene, which led me to the decision to have a double mastectomy. My surgery was scheduled the week before Christmas and I was struggling greatly with a vast amount of emotions over everything that was happening. I came home from the hospital on Christmas Eve with little to no use of my arms, but my family tried to make Christmas morning special by all wearing pink for me.

Fast forward, a year later. Christmas was once again upon us and I wanted this to be the Christmas I felt I lost the year before.

The first thing I did was to decorate my tree in pink! I filled the tree with pink ribbon, pink poinsettias and the only ornaments were ones from family. It was to celebrate the strength and love of our family that helped me through recovery, and to remember those who were still battling breast cancer.

The second thing I did was put together a basket of goodies for the nurses who cared for me at the hospital. I delivered the basket and asked if there was another woman there who was going through something similar. I was told there were a few women, so I put together a gift bag, decked myself out in pink and even wore a pink Santa hat (thanks to Victoria's Secret and my daughter), and went back to the hospital the next day for a visit. My gifts weren't much, but I was able to sit in a room and listen to one lady who was suffering her second round of breast cancer. I was thankful God gave me the opportunity to bless someone else, as it became my unexpected Christmas blessing that year!

 ## How I Got Through It

The support of my family and church family was tremendous. The Sunday before my surgery, unbeknownst to me, everyone in the church wore pink and decked the front of the church in pink poinsettias. They provided meals for us for a month after my surgery as well.

 ## Action Items

Embrace the pink! Plan a way to support someone else who may be experiencing the same challenge as you have already faced. Make a note in the Yearbook page as to how you will carry out this plan.

Yearbook

_____

_____

_____

_____

_____

_____

_____

_____

_____

_____

_____

_____

_____

_____

_____

_____

_____

_____

_____

_____

_____

_____

_____

_____

_____

_____

_____

_____

_____

_____

_____

_____

Kefir, Kvass, and Kontrol

Cathy Donaldson

*"And he said to his disciples, 'Therefore I tell you, do not
be anxious about your life, what you will eat, nor about
your body, what you will put on. For life is more than food,
and the body more than clothing. Consider the ravens:
they neither sow nor reap, they have neither storehouse
nor barn, and yet God feeds them. Of how much more
value are you than the birds! And which of you by being
anxious can add a single hour to his span of life? If then
you are not able to do as small a thing as that, why are
you anxious about the rest?'" ~Luke 12:22-26 (ESV)*

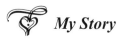 *My Story*

Okay, so right up front let me just confess—I like control. I don't idolize it
or go too crazy about it. But, oh man, I sure do like it. It fuels organization,
and I really *really* like organization. It makes our household run smoothly.
It makes me look like a hero to my husband or kids when I find some
beloved something for them.

I like the control part of meal planning, especially for the kids. Healthy
food, balanced diet, carefully chosen supplements. I have been known to
sneak kale and beets into smoothies. A few tomatoes and an avocado get
pureed into just about everything. We drink raw milk. I make homemade

kefir on my kitchen countertop. Once, I even made beet kvass. I admit it was gross, but I haven't given up on it completely. The emphasis is on "healthy in." You get the idea.

The incredible irony of chemotherapy in my very near future has not escaped my notice. In less than one week, I will be a regular partaker of toxic fluids, and I will be doing it on purpose, praying that I stay on schedule so I can get the maximum dosage. One of my doctors jokingly calls it "jet fuel." That seems pretty close to the truth to me right about now. My semi-paleo, nourishing traditions, whole foods brain is shrieking in protest. Can't they make a chemotherapy that is labeled "Organic"?

 ### *How I Got Through It*

I read the verse that emphasized not being anxious about your life and examines what you will put in your body, and I realize this is the time the rubber meets the road. Those words are nice in theory, but I thought, "Do I really believe them? Do I really have enough faith to not be anxious? Do I really believe that I am so valuable to God that I can ingest 'jet fuel' with confidence in Him?"

It is then, asking myself those questions, that I remember Whose I am yet again. And I remember that I cannot add any hours to a life I didn't make in the first place. The control is not mine: it is His. He knows my future. Since I trust God about the big things like salvation and absolute truth and my marriage and my children, surely I can trust Him about chemotherapy. Surely.

 ### *Action Items*

What are *you* anxious about? What circumstances in your life do you try hard to control? What would it take for you to yield those circumstances up to the One who loves you best? Take a moment to reflect on these questions and record your thoughts in the Yearbook page that follows.

Yearbook

Why?

Lucinda West

*"I know God won't give me anything I can't handle, I
just wish He didn't trust me so much." ~Mother Teresa*

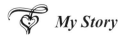 *My Story*

I'm no Mother Teresa. I admit I had a few moments of "sulking" during
my cancer treatment. While my perspective hadn't changed in that I knew
God was in control, I would be kidding myself if I said that every moment
was filled with silver linings and pixie dust. Just like any other human
diagnosed with cancer, the question of "why" occurred more than once.
As the date of my mastectomy drew closer, and doctor visits increased in
frequency, I had on more than one occasion asked this one-word question
in my internal dialogue with the Lord.

On a pursuit to answer this question, I looked to heroes in the Bible. I
discovered that Job, a man who lost everything including his health, asked
why. Yet God never answered this query. In effect He said, *"Who are you
to question me?"* (my paraphrase) and then orated a lengthy lecture about
His power and sovereign nature versus Job's puny insight and mortality. I
don't know about you, but I don't want a lecture from God. I want to trust
His insight, even if I don't fully understand or agree with it.

Even so, sometimes I asked why. Human nature seeks to strip away the mystery from God. We want to figure it all out, logically or scientifically explain the supernatural. Yet He reminded me to just have faith, knowing that He had it all in control.

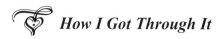 *How I Got Through It*

Having this diagnosis put a lot of past events into perspective, and even provided a sense of closure to some as well. The Lord has taught me important lessons through each major life event—lessons that would help me through an even greater crisis than the one before—lessons that would help me deal with breast cancer. At the moment each crisis occurred, I questioned why. In retrospect, it makes sense.

I am comforted in knowing that each event has made me who I am today. Each crisis has prepared me for handling this moment. I was not blind-sided by a diagnosis of cancer and impending treatment because the trials I have faced in life provided me a foundation for dealing with future challenges. I had learned to totally depend on God, and I needed Him now more than ever.

I now have a much greater understanding of God's perspective. His vision is not myopic. He sees the whole picture and life process across eternal time and space, spanning millions of people and priorities. While He could change our immediate circumstance, He has a reason for not doing so. We may not ever apprehend the reason *why*. But knowing that He has our best interest at heart, understands our future, and holds our future in His hands is comforting. Relying on Him gives me peace, because only He can simultaneously see past, present, future, and eternity.

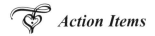 *Action Items*

Have you been asking the question why? Write the word "why" in the Yearbook page that follows. Then cross it out and write the words, "I accept." Ask God to help you in your journey toward acceptance, as you trust in Him. Now journal any thoughts you may have to help change your "why" to "I accept." For further reflection, read Job 38:1–42:6.

Yearbook

Passions In Life

Frances Schlueter

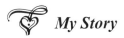 *My Story*

A simple question challenged my thinking and ended up pushing me to start living a more fulfilling life: What is your passion?

My journey as a two-time breast cancer survivor started when I was 45 years old, and it dismantled the world that I lived in. I lost my job after becoming too ill to continue working, and I have never been able to return to work. At this writing I am 54 years old, and after several years of nonstop medical intervention, I am cancer-free and finally feeling well. Now that I was no longer ill, or spending all my time in treatment and recovery, I began to look for ways to fill the empty space.

I found a lot of little, busy things to occupy my time, but none of them were fulfilling. How do you replace a career that you thought, someday, you would retire from? I thought I was preparing myself in my career for an empty nest, but instead, my nest emptied while I was sick and my husband still traveled. Clearly, I had not planned for this and was at a loss on how to proceed.

I read books and searched the Internet, looking for ways to fill my time. Not knowing what I was searching for, I came up empty handed over and over again. At my very next visit, my oncologist innocently asked me how I spending days now that wellness was on the horizon. I could only answer with tears. Word of encouragement and reassurance were followed with a question that stumped me. "What is your passion?" I drew a blank. I could not think of anything. Before I knew it, I had an assignment—find my passion by the next visit. This would be easy enough, or so I thought.

Over coffee the next afternoon, I sat down with a pad of paper to write down my passions. I wrote down 'reading,' and then I just sat there. Surely there was more to my life than just reading. What did I love? In the days and weeks to follow, I was shocked to learn that I did not really have any passions beyond reading. Clearly, passions were more than just interests or hobbies.

I began asking people around me what their passions were and everyone could spontaneously rattle off several. I became fixated on the concept and thought about it nonstop. Somehow, I had let life pass me by without ever finding something in life that I was passionate about! Not only did I not have a passion, I did not know how to find one. At my next appointment with my oncologist, I reported on my struggle to find my passion. We laughed as we discussed how you don't find it by looking on the Internet, but instead by being open to what was going on in the world around you.

 ## *How I Got Through It*

Since that discussion, I have opened my eyes to the world of possibilities around me and have pushed myself outside of my comfort zone. I have signed up for book clubs, tried new exercise classes, cooked new recipes, explored the world around me, and focused on learning new things. I am zeroing in on potential passions in life and no longer feel intimidated by my search. Never again will I answer, "nothing" when asked about what I am doing with my life.

 *Action Items*

What are you passionate about? Write the word "passion" on the Yearbook page that follows, and randomly list ideas as they come to you. Don't judge the ideas; just write them down. Then pick one to explore more in-depth within the next few weeks.

Yearbook

Wigs for Fun

Anonymous

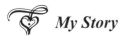 *My Story*

I took my son shopping. This was no ordinary shopping trip, as we were buying a wig. He was six at the time. This was our special time together as I also had two little girls back at home. I remember standing at the center of the store with him looking at all the wigs, wondering what was going on in his little mind. I didn't want him to worry, so I never shared with him my cancer journey. He thought we were here shopping just for fun, so we made a game out of it. He still thinks I bought a wig because I wanted to, not because I was losing my hair.

Having three young children while going through this journey has been challenging. I still had a toddler at home when I received my diagnosis, and she demanded much of my time. My children were six, four, and 18-months old.

 *How I Got Through It*

I smile when my 18-month old daughter remembers me after I've been away for a long day at work. I never want her to forget me. I see the smile on her face and believe she knows who I am. My deepest goal is to be here and live long enough for my youngest to remember me. That keeps me going, gives me the strength I need to make it through my regular treatments, and it makes each day important to me. I maintain a positive mental attitude, keep going, and spend as much time with my children as I can.

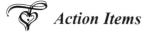 **Action Items**

Spend time with your loved ones whenever you can. Continue to make good memories and pass on words of wisdom and life lessons to your family and friends. You may do something as simple as enjoying a meal, discussing or reading books together, watching a movie, singing songs, dancing, telling jokes, going to a park, baking or cooking, running through a sprinkler, starting a scrapbook and yes, even shopping for wigs.

Record some ideas for family fun or reflect on your own activities in the Yearbook page that follows.

Yearbook

Fight For My Life

Karen Dion

"Honey, you're gonna out-live me!" ~my husband.

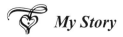 *My Story*

I knew from the beginning this fight was going to be an uphill battle. I collected all my resources quickly, and I mentally and spiritually prepared myself to fight for my life. The enemy (lobular carcinoma) was sneaky and undetectable by most standard technologies available. Twenty-seven mammograms and four core biopsies could not detect the enemy already occupying my body. A determined surgeon out-smarted the machinery with a bilateral lumpectomy, which finally confirmed the devastating news. Ready or not, the fight was on.

Recruitment included my church community, family, neighbors, doctors, nurses and cancer survivors to help me win this war. What happened next was amazing! Recruits willingly showed up and in most cases without asking. The word spread quickly and I let it take its course. It goes against every cell in my body to let others take control of the details of my life and my family's, but I knew I needed an army. The neighborhood ladies rallied to the battle with an opening "Bra Burning Party." My church community barricaded and fortified the fort by setting up a support group, which provided news from the front lines, meals and house cleaning.

My family and daughter were always available with words of encouragement, smiles, hugs and kisses. My husband was, and continues to be, my rock, scout and reinforcement. He is always prepared for every battle and constantly present. And he comes equipped with a sense of humor bigger than a house. The double mastectomy left me with two round scars where my nipples used to be, a round scar around my belly button and a slightly upward curved scar across my abdomen from hip to hip. The enemy left me with a permanent happy face! So after winning this long drawn out battle, that's something to smile about!

 ## How I Got Through It

My faith in God and people helped me get through this experience. I witnessed human kindness and love at its core through family, friends, the medical community and complete strangers. Suffering has meaning and this witness of love is a grace from God.

"Do not be afraid" is the opening statement in quite a few of the Mysteries of the Rosary. I counted on this everyday! I made time at the end of each day for an hour of prayer and meditation. This helped me immensely, and still does!

I learned to put my life unconditionally in the hands of the Lord and pray the Rosary often, for spiritual, physical and mental strength. This is the most important single ritual I still do daily, because it keeps me focused on the purpose of suffering and life. I did not say the Rosary very often (if at all) before the cancer discovery process. Now, I think of it as my anti-depressant!

 ## Action Items

If you are reading this story, you have made a commitment to fight the cancer within you. You are to be commended for your determination.

Make a battle plan with only one goal: winning. Reach out and let others help you. Like God's angels tell us (from the Mysteries of the Rosary), "Don't be afraid!" Take a moment to write about your battle plan in the Yearbook page that follows.

Yearbook

An Unexpected Journey

DeLann Johnson

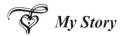 *My Story*

I was operating a day care at the time I received my breast cancer diagnoses. I had to make a decision as to whether to close operations or try and keep everything as normal as possible until the end of the school year. After much thought and prayer, I decided to keep it open.

When my hair started to fall out I began wearing a scarf. The kids just looked at me with priceless expressions on their faces as they tried to figure out why I was suddenly wearing something on my head. The four-year-old children wanted me to take the "hat" off so they could see my head. So, one day I explained that my hair was falling out but that it would grow back soon. They wanted to see! So I showed them. Some stared; some giggled; and some just downright laughed.

The day I started wearing my wig was another precious day. I picked the children up from school and their reactions were delightful. Sam, the oldest just kept staring and trying to figure out what was different about me. When I asked Tanner if he liked my new hair, he replied with a simple "no." Preston and Rylee had quizzical expressions on their faces, and I asked them what they were looking at. Rylee, age three, just said, "Hair." Roslyn, also three, told me I looked beautiful. That girl has always had good taste!

How I Got Through It

From the very beginning I made a conscious decision that I would be positive and open during the journey of mine. A positive attitude is sometimes the best medicine and I sure wanted the best medicine for my body, mind, and soul. Secondly, I didn't want anyone to be uncomfortable around me, especially the children. So, I informed everyone they could ask me anything about my cancer. I would answer their questions to the best of my ability. This allowed everyone to be themselves and not worry about upsetting me with questions.

The most important thing that truly got me through this journey was prayer and knowing that no matter the outcome, I had God on my side. Immediately after the doctor confirmed the cancer, a good friend of mine said, "Let's pray." An inner peace came over my body. Whether things turned out like I wanted them to or not, I knew God was there for me, and He would give me strength to make it one day at a time.

Once my family and friends knew my diagnosis, the phone calls and emails started coming in droves. This made me feel loved and gave me so much needed encouragement. However, after repeatedly telling the same stories of how I discovered my breast cancer, treatment protocols, how was I feeling, and attempting to answer everyone's questions, I started emailing my journal to keep everyone apprised of the progress in my unexpected journey. I had so many people tell me how much they looked forward to my journey emails and how they appreciated me sharing my thoughts and feelings with them. As my treatments progressed and my body was not holding up as well, this method of sharing made it much easier on me.

Action Items

Take a moment and reflect in the Yearbook page below on the following. How might you share your journey with your family and friends without spending too much additional energy of your own? Also take a moment to write down the pros and cons of working or taking off work. What activities can you put on hold to provide time for treatment?

Yearbook

Igor

Lucinda West

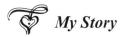 *My Story*

Enter Igor. That's not completely accurate, really, and of course it is not his real name. In reality he was a very nice gentleman and tried to make me laugh on more than one occasion. He treated me professionally and explained each step of the procedure. Subsequent actions, however, reminded me of the evil scientist's assistant as he stretched my arm to an extremely painful position, told me to "hold the pose" for 30 minutes, marked my body for treatment, scanned me in and out of the CT machine, and gave me my first set of tattoos. Yes, I now have tattoos, although they may not count as such to those who have a "real" tattoo of a butterfly, pretty flower, or skull and crossbones. Four little permanent dots now mark the treatment spots in the event the red Sharpie wears off over the next six weeks.

I say he "tried" to make me laugh because his eastern European humor was a little off-beat. English is his second language and I enjoyed talking with him about Krakow, Budapest, Bratislava and other eastern European cities we have both visited. After the marking session was complete, Igor asked with his slight Polish accent, "So what will you say now when people ask you if you have any tattoos?"

Me, somewhat hesitant: "Well, I guess I do now?"

Him: "And when they ask you if they can see your tattoo, you can tell them no. Tell them to use their imagination and connect the dots."

 ## *How I Got Through It*

Radiation is a daily experience, and it can be quite tiring. Igor helped me to see the humor in an otherwise difficult situation. I decided to find humorous ways to help me make it through the daily grind. My teenage daughter laughed out loud when I shared this story with her on the way out to the parking lot. It was a bonding moment for us. We had an hour for lunch before my next appointment so we went to our favorite café. There was a prominent Sharpie mark in the middle of my chest, which my shirt failed at hiding. It was interesting to watch the expressions of people who noticed.

I became much more open to whatever the technicians and doctors threw my way. I never thought I would be brave enough to get a tattoo, and here I was getting my first. No matter what I faced, I knew I would make it through! And, I planned to have a laugh or two along the journey.

 ## *Action Items*

Have you been through radiation? If so, how will you answer people when they ask if you have any tattoos? Can you think of a humorous response to give them? If you did not require radiation, how has this story helped you to become more aware of others who have? It you were to get a tattoo, what would it look like? Draw a fun picture and color it in, then write your response to some of these questions in the Yearbook page below.

Yearbook

Retreat

Anonymous

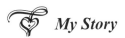 *My Story*

I was 35 years old when I was diagnosed with breast cancer. It came as a shock because I had no known risk factors associated with the exception of a late first pregnancy. I never thought I would have to worry about breast cancer.

At the time of my diagnosis I had a toddler at home who would not understand I needed rest. In a way this was good because my daughter kept me going, but it was challenging as well. My daughter didn't usually watch TV. However, after my treatment began, I would make her watch TV so I could get a mere 30 minutes of rest. Due to my busy lifestyle as a part-time physician, there wasn't a day I could just put my feet up and relax. At times it felt like I was riding on a roller coaster. I didn't have time to think. I just kept going and doing what I needed to do. However, it would hit me when I was going to my appointments that I really had cancer. During those moments of waiting I decide to make this a time to indulge myself. I pictured these days like a day at the spa. This was my retreat.

 How I Got Through It

As I was lying on the table during the numerous PET scans, MRIs and other tests, I would close my eyes and rest. I welcomed these opportunities to be by myself. I decided to view these moments as a relief from my daily responsibilities. This helped me get through it, as I envisioned these times as a respite, rather than an intrusion into my busy life. Being a physician I often wanted to help out (and lots of opportunities presented themselves), but I learned the importance of setting limits and taking care of myself. Now I back off from these external pressures so I can take care of me as well as spend what precious time I have with my children.

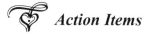 ***Action Items***

Maintaining a positive mental attitude is critical during treatment. This is the time when it's okay to focus on you, however contrary to our innate female nature. View your appointments as a retreat instead of an intrusion. Use the time with more purpose. Arrive early and relax your body before entering the testing fields. Pull out a good book or your favorite music while you wait. Tell yourself it's okay to be a little selfish and take care of you. Record your thoughts about how you might retreat in the Yearbook page that follows.

❦ *Yearbook*

_____

_____

_____

_____

_____

_____

_____

_____

_____

_____

_____

_____

_____

_____

_____

_____

_____

_____

_____

_____

_____

_____

_____

_____

_____

_____

_____

_____

_____

_____

_____

_____

Maintenance

Janet Cable

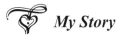 *My Story*

My mother had cancer too. I was real nervous about radiation for my breast cancer because she had it back in the 1980s when technology was less advanced, and I remember what she went through. But my radiation oncologist told me I should be fine. She said the lighter your skin is, the better it would be. I didn't believe her because I always got sunburned wherever I went. It didn't make sense to me, but she was right! I didn't have any trouble with the radiation. I worked the whole time, and it didn't even make me tired.

One thing I do remember which helped me through each radiation session: A team of four shared the rotation and gave me my treatment. They did what they could to keep it light-hearted and to calm my nerves. The very first day I went in I was so nervous, and I asked the technician if he had done this before. I was just trying to make conversation and I didn't expect what came next. He leaned over and whispered in my ear, "Last week I was flipping hamburgers at McDonald's. I'm just starting out." That broke the ice and I felt much better from then on.

 *How I Got Through It*

I was talking to one patient who was also waiting for his radiation, and he said he had about seven different kinds of cancers. He said he goes in regularly for treatment, and has "maintenance" done. He said it's just like a car, but we have maintenance done on our bodies.

We all do that, whether it's our teeth or our hair—we have maintenance. I would get real nervous before my mammogram, but I kept reminding myself, "this is just maintenance," and it helped me calm down. This perspective abated my anxiety.

 *Action Items*

Breast cancer is not what it used to be. It doesn't have to be a death sentence. People from Stage 0 through Stage IV have survived cancer and continue to live long and productive lives. No matter what stage you are in, keep that hope in front of you, knowing there is survivorship on the other side. When you go in for treatment, try to remember: it is just "maintenance." Write about some maintenance you have had on your body recently, and how you coped.

Yearbook

Live Every Day!

Pam Criss

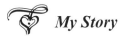 *My Story*

My cancer journey began at the age of 56 one morning in early August when I felt a lump in my breast after waking up. Surely it was nothing! After all, I had a mammogram five months earlier and it was clear. I went to my doctor anyway and his actions quickly confirmed my suspicion that this was something to be concerned about. By the time the biopsy report came, I was diagnosed with Stage IIB breast cancer.

I dissolved into tears. Within another week, a PET scan showed evidence that I actually had IIIC, later confirmed as stage IV. I was determined to do whatever I had to do to stay alive. The first chemotherapy treatment knocked the fool out of me and I was temporarily ready to resign. But I pressed on with the help of a faithful husband, supportive family, and coworkers by my side. After 20 weeks of chemotherapy, surgery, and 33 radiation treatments, I was relieved to get an "all clear" a mere eight months later.

I joked that they tried to kill me—first, they poisoned me; then they cut me; then they burned me—all in the name of healing. Today, I still get a preventative treatment every three weeks. Oddly enough, going to the chemotherapy lab gives me a sense of calm. It is a place where healing takes place. I am incredibly grateful for the expertise and skill of my doctors!

How I Got Through It

There were so many factors that helped me survive the initial diagnosis and treatments that followed. First, I have a precious faith in a God who loves me. I don't understand why things like this happen, but I am 100% confident that He can see the whole plan. And one of these days, I'll have a chance to talk to Him about this while we are spending eternity together. At that point, all of the things of this Earth won't really matter anymore.

Second, quitting was never an option for me. I like my life and I am fiercely determined to do all that I can to have more days on this Earth. I knew I had to press on and continue with the plan.

Third, I value my family and friends who helped me to get through treatment. Sixty hot meals made life much easier, so that I could concentrate on survival. A large box full of cards and letters will never be thrown away, as they remind me of what encouragement can do.

Fourth, I did what I was physically able to do whenever I could. During the worst regime of chemotherapy, we managed a three-day trip to the beach. One week before surgery, we ventured to New Orleans and braved the freezing weather to see a Mardi Gras parade. My husband and I were committed to celebrating whenever we could, regardless of the circumstances.

Action Items

The gift of cancer is that you *know* that life can be short—too short to take one day for granted. This allows us to be in a very special club of people who can revel in the gifts of the present day. I count my todays. As of this writing, I have lived an incredible 1,265 todays. How many todays have you lived?

What if I had accepted a Stage IV diagnosis as a death sentence and failed to enjoy those days? That would have been a complete waste! I choose joy! I choose to live every day! Choose to live each day with joy and a spirit of adventure. Write about living in the Yearbook page that follows.

Yearbook

Positively Radiant

Cathy Donaldson

Two atoms are sitting in a field of ionizing radiation. One atom says, "I think I lost an electron." The other says, "Are you sure?" The first atom says, "I'm positive!"

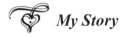 *My Story*

Here's how radiation treatment goes...

1. I walk in (or rather, run in, because I am usually behind schedule).
2. I smile at the man at the check-in desk and he doesn't even ask my name anymore.
3. I zip to the back of the office, grab a gown out of the drawer, slip it on, and unceremoniously stuff my bra and shirt into my purse (except for the day I forgot to take my bra off… that got a laugh from the treatment crew).
4. I slip on my medical wristband and get out my radiation ID card (it is sort of like an amusement park Season Pass, only way more expensive and a lot less thrilling).
5. I walk around the corner and usually the radiation ladies are smiling and waving me into the room. I climb onto the table and adjust myself into a foam cradle that was form-fitted to my body. We chat about kids and workouts and weekend plans while they adjust me to line up the green grid lines coming from the ceiling with the lines on my breast (I've got several lines of blue Sharpie

on and around my right breast. I've told my husband I might do up the left side to match and look like some tribal-ish war-paint thingy, but so far it just doesn't seem that funny—or sexy—to either of us).

6. The radiation ladies leave the room and the treatments bursts begin. The metal pieces in the machine shift around to restrict the radiation field. The machine rotates to the other side for more bursts. During the bursts, I try to lay as still as possible and imagine all the cancer cells in my body clamoring to get to my breast, where the radiation blast nails them, sort of like a low-budget video game.

7. I get dressed, collect my Season Pass, and go home.

 How I Got Through It

Keep plugging away, day after day! Don't give up. Smile at people. Look in their eyes. Engage in their lives. Laugh at good jokes. Laugh at the bad ones too!

 Action Items

Is there anything you take too seriously? Who shares that burden with you? Can you try, even just once, to make a joke about it? Write about something silly, or draw a cartoon in the Yearbook page below.

Yearbook

Life After Cancer

Margaret Looper

"He must become greater; I must become less." ~John 3:30

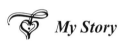 *My Story*

I remember when a good day was a day no one was sticking me with a needle. As the days, weeks, and now years have flown by since my cancer treatment, I think about life after cancer. I have developed into a "new normal." I have grown to realize that each moment of life is precious—a beautiful gift to share. Cancer taught me so many valuable lessons. I will list a few for you to ponder.

1. Pause and listen; appreciate the songs of birds.
2. Let God's love for you shine through your face, and smile.
3. Lose yourself by doing for others.
4. Look for Jesus in each person you encounter.
5. Look for ways to fill your heart with joy.
6. Be thankful for everything.

 How I Got Through It

During treatment, it is easy to become the center of your universe. Keeping up with appointments, suffering from reactions, loss of hair, etc. can cause you to think only about yourself. A brief glance in the mirror can bring tears and self-pity will often follow. The best way to rid yourself of focusing on yourself every moment is to focus on others. Treat yourself with kindness, and then do for others something even kinder. Think of ways to help someone who is less fortunate than you are.

I remember wondering, if I survived cancer, *what was I going to do with the rest of my life?* This is an important question for everyone to answer, but was especially relevant to me as I fought this disease. That is when I decided to start volunteering at the cancer center where I received treatment. Volunteering is simply serving others from the heart. That has been my way to serve others. Cancer has made me a better person.

 ## *Action Items*

As we focus on God and helping others, it takes the focus off of our circumstances. Take a look at this verse from the book of John listed above, and think about how you might focus on giving God glory by doing something for others. Write the name of one person you could help, or decide which thirty minutes you could give to volunteer your time. Reflect on your experience in the Yearbook page that follows.

❦ Yearbook

Keeping the Faith in Trying Days

Brenda Putnam

"You're going to be just fine. God's got this." ~A friend

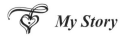 *My Story*

Determined to make lemonade of the "Big Lemon," I insisted on keeping a positive attitude and did several things to help myself, and possibly others. I kept a journal of each session and medical appointment that included how I felt, side effects, and something I learned. This went into a binder along with handouts of information given to me. During the months of chemotherapy, I wrote a document of tips and helps to share with other cancer patients. I shared my experiences about hair, head covers, hands-feet-skin care, taste changes, and how to create a binder.

After completing chemotherapy, I soon began 30 days of radiation. I loved meeting with my radiation buddies in the waiting area and laughing and sharing, doing my best to encourage smiles and positive feelings. We were in different places with different cancers but we had a commonality and sisterhood that helped us survive the treatments. When all was finished, thanks to the generosity of an old friend, I celebrated recovery with my husband in Hawaii for a much-needed week of rest and restoration.

This journey has made me realize how short life is and how insignificant too many things are in our lives. I have learned to focus more on positive relationships and to be more selective about how my energy is spent.

How I Got Through It

Two Scriptures helped me be at peace. Proverbs 31:25 says "She is clothed with strength and dignity; she can laugh at the days to come." After receiving the diagnosis, I was devastated, especially since I had annual mammograms. But this scripture told me to be strong and courageous, not afraid of what might happen, because God is on my side. I even added it to my email signature.

The second is Philippians 3:19, "Do not be anxious about anything, but in everything by prayer and supplication with thanksgiving let your requests be made known to God. And the peace of God, which surpasses all understanding, will guard your hearts and your minds in Christ Jesus." Although difficult, I turned my worries over to God because He is the only one who can give me peace, knowing everything is in His control. I claimed that supernatural strength and peace for myself. In addition to spiritual nourishment, I was blessed with neighbors who fed us and helped transport me to treatments when my husband was unavailable.

Action Items

How important do you think mental outlook is to your wellness? What interests, hobbies, or talents do you have that can be adapted/shared to serve you or others during treatments for illness? Respond to these questions in the Yearbook page that follows as you reflect on the story above.

Yearbook

Business as Usual?

Lucinda West

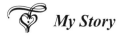 *My Story*

I just got back from a business trip up north—an annual conference for work. I debated with myself on whether I should go. After all, I justified, I have been on chemotherapy for about six weeks now. I would have been excused, and I would have had a good reason!

I thought back to what my medical oncologist said. She wants me to live as "normal" a life as possible, and she doesn't want chemotherapy to get in the way of living. I wasn't on the hard chemotherapies yet, so my platelets were fine. I decided to go.

TSA patted my head down on the way up, as my cranial prosthesis (wig) was glowing on their security screen. I had flown many times before, but this was a first for me. The conference attendees provided additional pats and hair flips, or at least a mention of my distinguishing hair traits. I was more guarded than usual, and felt vulnerable, fearful someone might accidentally pull it and it would slide uneven, or worse yet, fall off.

I decided to keep my wig a secret. It is intriguing how many conversations (for women, anyway) center around hair. It's even more entertaining when you are wearing a wig. "I love your hair," or "do you use a flat iron?" or "I like the way you part your hair." Then there was my favorite: the awkward pause when a co-worker noticed out loud that my hair looks different, cocked her head to the side with a quizzical look as though she wanted to say something further but stopped herself. I wondered what she was thinking, but I didn't encourage her to go on for fear of embarrassing her in the process.

It wasn't just "business as usual." I became much more in tune to the possible situations people were bringing with them from their homes and personal lives. Conceivably they had secrets as well. No one would know. Perhaps they were covering something up in the same way I was. I am more sensitive of the people who surround me now, and I am more attentive to listen to their spirits as they speak.

 ## How I Got Through It

I didn't go to the conference prepared with a "hair" speech, so I typically just nodded my head in agreement. No one asked, and I didn't tell. My diagnosis is not a secret, but at this point I chose to keep my work and personal lives in separate silos. This helped me get through it, and helped me feel a little more "normal" at the meetings.

While feeling physically spent, attending the conference actually revitalized my perspective. I was invited to stand up twice and be recognized by our CAO for efforts by my team. It was magical, and I pondered a lot. Further, it didn't get in the way of my Thursday chemotherapy.

 ## Action Items

Think about how you might take care of yourself while you are undergoing treatment. Will you continue to work, or cut back on the hours? Travel or stay home? In the Yearbook page below, write about one thing you could do for self-care.

In addition, here's a fun comment/discussion starter: Take the next day or two and observe how many "hair" conversations you notice at work, home, at the grocery store, and in general with the people you meet.

🎗 *Yearbook*

_____
_____
_____
_____
_____
_____
_____
_____
_____
_____
_____
_____
_____
_____
_____
_____
_____
_____
_____
_____
_____
_____
_____
_____
_____
_____
_____

Hair Loss and a Young Family

Rachel Livingston

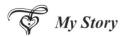 *My Story*

On a Monday afternoon I received the call: "You have breast cancer." The next day I was shuffled from a surgeon to an oncologist where I was told, "You will lose your hair." I was to start chemotherapy nine days later, and I was told I would have 10-14 days after that until my hair fell out. It all happened so quickly. I was in denial. My mother had breast cancer and she didn't lose her hair! Maybe I had her great genes! Oh how little I knew about breast cancer types and treatment techniques.

Other than the blow of cancer, the blow of appearance change hit me even harder at the time. I had just turned 29 the month before the diagnosis. This was to be the best year of my life! I was already actively working on getting my "body back" after two children. I had big plans to look my best *ever* by my 30th birthday and to celebrate with a well-deserved tropical vacation with my husband. Instead, I was facing hair loss, breast amputation, and radiation induced skin damage. Although I had faith that I'd beat this cancer, I couldn't control my vanity… the idea that breast cancer was going to steal my youth and beauty.

Scared as I was to lose my hair, I wondered about the fear my children might feel watching my appearance change too quickly and drastically. I had a six-year old and a 20-month old baby. Would this traumatize them for life? When my hair started to fall out, I stood in front of the mirror crying for three days, pulling my hair out in clumps.

How I Got Through It

Finally, my husband had to shake me out of it. "You're losing your hair and driving yourself crazy. *It's time to accept it.*" That's when we decided to shave my head. We determined to turn this into a fun and bonding experience with the kids. That Saturday night we got out the clippers, razors, and watercolors! My husband shaved his head with me, and we even let my son help buzz my head. Once my head was bald, we allowed the kids to get messy and use the water colors to finger paint my head! I am proud of how we turned a traumatic experience into something we all will remember as a moment that brought us together as a family.

Breast cancer attempts to steal so much from you. It steals time with your family, your health, dignity, sense of fairness, body parts, appearance, and so on. However, I wasn't going to concentrate on the losses. I personally dealt with the baldness yet another way a few months later. I was so tired of looking at my bare head. I never wore a wig, only hats or scarves in public. So I got the idea to have my head henna tattooed around Halloween time. I found a local artist and she spent hours painting my head. It was very therapeutic and for one of the first times in months, I felt beautiful.

 ### *Action Items*

Rather than focus on the losses, what can you do to make this awful experience "fun?" Make a memory with your loved ones that you know will outshine the darkness. Write about your experiences in the Yearbook page of this book.

Yearbook

Grace, Faith, and Hope

Vicky Conover

 *My Story*

After adopting two orphans from China (we named them Grace and Faith), we tried to adopt a third daughter. We would have named her Hope. Unfortunately, I was diagnosed with a callous and conscienceless brute named breast cancer, making me ineligible to adopt her at that time. So I pondered, *"Lord, what are you telling me?"*

He didn't answer me right away, but I later learned how my journey provided hope and saved the lives of other children.

In spite of my desire to do everything myself, I quickly realized I needed help. I had five children by this time, three boys and the two adopted girls, ranging from one to thirteen years old. It is okay to ask for help, or at least accept it when someone offers. Remember, you don't have to take care of everything yourself. The person God sends may be blessed by helping you.

A single woman with two grown boys came and cared for my five children while I was in Houston getting treatment. The Lord really spoke to her while she was living with me, as she watched the love I had for all my children. Subsequently, she determined she needed to become a foster parent. She said, "After I fell in love with your girls, I knew I could foster these kids." She did go on to become a foster mother, ultimately adopting her foster children. God used my circumstance to confirm what He wanted her to do with her life.

How I Got Through It

I made it through my breast cancer journey because I had five children who depended on me. The adoption process prompted me to do whatever I could to beat this disease. Those girls needed me. This knowledge gave me strength to move forward. I felt like I needed to be there, alive, for everybody.

That summer before I was diagnosed with breast cancer, I read a Bible study about hope. I truly believed we would adopt a third daughter and name her Hope. After learning we could not adopt the little girl we had been supporting, I discussed this with the Lord. He taught me that hope was what I needed to carry me through the next journey in my life. I wouldn't have a child named Hope, but I *would* have hope.

Action Items

What does God have in store for your life? Perhaps He will use your breast cancer journey to help others. Ask the Lord to instill a sense of calling, a mission, a purpose, and He will provide the faith, grace and hope to see it through. Write your thoughts in the Yearbook page that follows.

Yearbook

The Things They Don't Tell You

Lucinda West

*"The thief comes only to steal and kill and
destroy; I have come that they may have life,
and have it to the full." ~John 10:10*

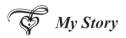 *My Story*

Maybe it's in the paperwork, but reading it there is not nearly as memorable as when it actually happens. The little twinge of "I've got to go" quickly moves to the "oh no, am I going to make it?" I thought only old ladies and babies had bladder control issues, but apparently this goes for chemotherapy patients as well. Now I understand why the clinic has signs in every restroom stall, offering to provide help for those who have soiled their clothing. Fortunately it has never happened in public, and I have made it just in time, most of the time. While tempting, I drew the line at wearing *Depends*. I walked passed them in the store, but kept on walking. I decided to just sit closer to the restroom and visit it more frequently.

In spite of this pesky little side effect, I refused to sit at home doing nothing. Six days had passed since my first FEC treatment (described to me as the "hard" chemotherapy), and I was doing well. I felt so good over the weekend, and it was such a beautiful day that I met up with some photographers to shoot the Texas bluebonnets. It was April 2013. The wildflower population was hindered by two freezes that year, but the landscape was still beautiful. My daughter Elizabeth was fifteen at the time. She accompanied me and we met some new friends.

We visited a living history farm, set in the 1830s. Elizabeth loves the Victorian era, so it was a thrill for us both. Workers dressed in period clothing answered questions about life on the farm, all the while remaining in character. I was particularly attentive of the technology they lacked in the early 1800s, and I was thankful I live in our day and time where doctors know how to cure breast cancer. I imagined many women died without knowing the reason why. We have come a long way since then!

 ## How I Got Through It

One day at a time, I made a decision not to let cancer or treatment stop me from living. No matter how tired I was, I tried to find something I could do that pleased me, like taking pictures or going to see a movie with my family. I listened to the doctors and followed their advice, resting when I needed to, but activity kept my attitude in check.

I was exhausted after our weekend photo shoot, but it was a satisfying fatigue. I felt proud that I took advantage of my energy while I could, and I enjoyed life! Cancer acts like a thief, but I determined not to let it stop me from living life to the fullest.

 ## Action Items

Don't let cancer, or your treatment, prevent you from living! When you are tired, rest. Listen to your body. But don't lay there forever. Ask yourself if there is something you have been eager to do, but haven't done it because you are afraid or tired. Even if it is seemingly insignificant, make a commitment to put it on your calendar and do it. Write about the thing you want to do, or dream of doing, in the Yearbook page below, and share your stories with others so your spirit of adventure can inspire someone else as well.

Yearbook

This Journey Called Hope

Liz Jackson

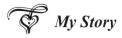 *My Story*

I didn't pray that it was not cancer, but I asked God to help me through it according to His perfect will for me. At age 65, I was diagnosed with invasive ductal carcinoma, stage II breast cancer. The surgeon told me I was *not* going to die from breast cancer. My response was, "Yes, I know!"

The following Sunday, I went to the altar at church to praise God for allowing me to discover the lump, and before the cancer spread to the lymph nodes. My pastor said, "If it's okay with you, we'll pray for your healing too!"

Following a lumpectomy, I was scheduled for 37 radiation treatments. I dreaded going to MD Anderson in downtown Houston five days a week. But, God had a plan. MD Anderson had just opened a satellite clinic five miles from my home! My radiation oncologist was compassionate and reassuring. In October, she asked for someone to speak about breast cancer at an assisted living facility, so I volunteered. As I stood before those precious ladies to talk about hope through breast cancer, I recognized that they just wanted to play bingo—they had their bingo cards and were ready to play when I finished talking! I also pondered whether most of them would ever have another mammogram due to their age and station in life. I was uncertain why I was speaking to this group of ladies. Again, God had a plan.

The director of the facility spoke next about her own breast cancer experience the previous year. Then she introduced her mother who had just been diagnosed as well. When I gave her mother a hug and spoke reassuring words to her, she pointed to the beautiful pink ribbon pin that I wore. Realizing that she spoke no English, and I spoke no Spanish, I took off that beautiful pin and pinned it on her. We needed no words to communicate God's love and compassion! That's when I understood why God had put me there—the one person who understood my message didn't even speak the same language!

 ## How I Got Through It

One of my doctors said to me, "I'm a Christian, and I know that you are too." My faith in God gave me hope, and the prayers of others sustained me. Medical research and technology gave me hope. More facilities for treating and "making cancer history" are now available outside metropolitan areas, and provided the treatment I needed just a few miles from home. I thank God for these tiny miracles. We have come a long way!

Joni Eareckson Tada, quadriplegic since her teenage years, was diagnosed with breast cancer a couple of years ago. Initially she thought it would be her ticket to Heaven. Instead, she received treatment and was cured. She continues to inspire me with these words: "I'm convinced that God is going to use our trials to stretch our faith, brighten our hope and strengthen our witness to others."

 ## Action Items

New treatment options for our specific needs are becoming available every year. Attend any seminars offered where doctors talk about new technologies and treatment options so you can learn from them. Also, surround yourself with family, friends, and encouragers. People want to help one another – let them help you. You can be the family, friend or encourager for someone else as well!

What will it take to strengthen your witness? Reflect on Joni Eareckson Tada's quote in the Yearbook page below.

Yearbook

Preconceived Thoughts
of Radiation

Tara Latta

"He will cover you with his feathers. He will shelter
you with his wings. His faithful promises are your
armor and protection." ~Psalm 91:4 (NLT)

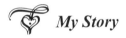 *My Story*

I am an optimist who loves life, but nerves get the best of me when doctors are involved and treatments are scheduled. When I heard that I would need to have radiation treatments for six weeks, many thoughts ran through my head about how bad the radiation was going to hurt during the treatment. Would the pain be unimaginable? How is this going to affect my daily life?

My preconceived thoughts of radiation were thankfully nothing of what I envisioned. My appointments always started with the comfort of the receptionist. She knew who I was and greeted me with a smile. I always felt at ease as I walked to the radiation sitting area where beautiful murals line the halls, soft music plays over the intercom, and of course, I was greeted by the friendly nurses and doctors we have all come to love. The waiting area offered a time and place to meet new people and get to know other patients as our appointments were usually scheduled at the same time each day.

The radiation team had a dynamic presence about them that brought calmness to me during my therapy. They treated me with compassion and respect while giving me the utmost diligent care. They made every step of radiation a smooth transition from taking my picture, getting tattoos, molding the head rest to fit me, and making me feel comfortable. The actual radiation treatments took less time than to change my clothes.

The radiation team never lets you feel alone while you're secluded in the radiation room. They use the intercom to speak to you and soothe your nerves. Amazingly, while the radiation machine is running, there is no direct pain. In such a short time, I grew to actually enjoy going for my appointments to visit with my newfound friends and the radiation team. When I reached my final treatment and rang the bell to signify I completed it, I had a hard time saying goodbye. This daily routine became a part of my life; in a weird way it brought me security knowing I was in the excellent care of the radiology team and physicians.

I am now a five-year cancer survivor. I am grateful radiation was a part of the cancer chapter in my life. Without cancer, I would not have been able to meet some incredible people that made a positive impact on my life.

How I Got Through It

I found myself on the same radiation schedule as a couple of other ladies. As we sat and waited our turn for treatments, we created a friendship. Others could hear us chatting and laughing through the halls. We would talk about how we were feeling, what we were experiencing, our families, and things of common interest. We were able to attend each other's bell ringing ceremony at the completion of radiation appointments. Years later, we still reconnect. No matter how long since our last visit, the memories are all so close.

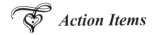

Action Items

Never underestimate the power of healing through friendship! Are nerves getting in your way of experiencing what is happening around you? Live in the moment. Breathe! Focus on life, and reflect on good friends. Don't be afraid to strike up a conversation with a patient sitting next to you. Write about your friends and good times in the Yearbook page that follows.

❦ *Yearbook*

Surgery Eve

Cathy Donaldson

"Jesus Christ is the same yesterday and
today and forever." ~Hebrews 13:8

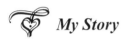 *My Story*

'Tis the night before surgery and all 'round our home; Are the piles and lists of things left undone. My laundry's still dirty; my bedroom's a sty. Every once in a while, my eyes get un-dry. Tomorrow we cut out this hideous stone; And pray its type be unambiguously known. We also pray hard that God's glory be shown; And He seed us liberally with mercies well sown. We love Him and trust Him and open our hand. Let His will be done in this Cancer-y Land.

* * *

My bedroom is a mess and I do need to toss in a load of laundry. I am not as ready as I hoped to be, but that is really just a function of externals at this point. I am ready on the inside, and that is the side that matters.

I am ready to get this cancer out!

And I am ready to be a wife, just like before (except better). And I am ready to be a mom, just like before (except better). And I am ready to be a friend, just like before (except better). Most of all, I am ready to be God's daughter, just like before (except better).

199

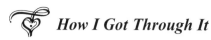

How I Got Through It

I would be a liar if I claimed to be fine with all of this. I am not. I am not looking forward to the anesthesia or pain or being drugged up or the inevitable constipation. I am not looking forward to what my breast will look like afterwards. I am not looking forward to watching my husband's face when he looks at it when the bandages come off the first time. I am not looking forward to my kids trying not to stare at me when I get out of the shower.

But ... We are okay. Rather than yielding to the ingratiating mood of the day, I am optimistically looking forward. I am looking forward to the next group of medical staff we will meet tomorrow. I look forward to what my risk-taking husband will say to them. I am looking forward to another day to glorify God. And I anticipate another day in the long chain of days of enjoying Him forever.

Yes. That. That is what I really need on this Surgery Eve. A glimpse of forever.

Action Items

When you look at the *forever* of your life, what do you see? As you prepare for surgery, think about things you can look forward to, and focus on those events in your life. Write your thoughts in the Yearbook page that follows.

Yearbook

Warding off Dracula

Lucinda West

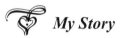 *My Story*

My humorous husband reminded me one day that I don't have to worry about vampires. One sniff of my chemo-infused blood would scare them off in less than a heartbeat. Can you envision it? One vampire says to the other, "Stay away from the bald ones—they taste horrible!" [Insert rimshot.]

One day was not so funny. I went to my medical oncologist for my routine follow-up and chemotherapy orders. So far I had not missed a treatment and the side effects were minimal. We were nearing the end of treatment and she called me a "rock star." Then she explained that my next dose would be delayed because my white blood cell counts were too low. *Delayed?!* I hated the sound of that word. It is interesting how you can have neutropenia and feel so good. I had to be extra careful not to expose myself to viruses or get sick. We nicknamed my condition "Count Dracula." We waited one week, and hoped my counts were back up where they needed to be.

On the one hand, I was glad to give my body a break. "Listen to your body," was the oncologist's advice. On the other hand, I just wanted to get the chemotherapy part over with so I could have surgery and eradicate this thing once and for all.

Thankfully, my white blood cell count came back normal at the next visit. It was not just normal enough for treatment, but "normal for anyone," she said.

Apparently once they start, white blood cells reproduce rather quickly. Our bodies are pretty amazing when you think about it. Our blood comes equipped with a million microscopic bodyguards; when they are killed off, they are capable of reproducing more bodyguards to prevent or heal our sickness. God is good and once again we saw evidence of prayers answered. I didn't get sick, and I was ready for the next treatment. Surgery was only delayed by one week.

 ## How I Got Through It

After shaking off the reality of the delay, I didn't let the fear of getting sick prevent me from living. I shook hands and hugged people at church, and I trusted God to keep me well. However, I didn't throw caution to the wind either. If someone was coughing, I steered clear. I avoided the medicine aisle as well as children with sniffles.

After my chemotherapy treatment, I took the rest of the day off, as well as the next day. Monday was a holiday so I had a nice long weekend to recuperate. My boss applauded me noting, "You haven't missed a beat." Working full time helped me stay distracted so I could get through the treatment process. It gave me something positive to focus on. However, work is work, and it can wait. I learned to put things into perspective and take time off when I needed the rest. Knowing I had the option of resting actually helped me complete my work and stay productive.

 ## Action Items

Don't overdo it! Listen to your body. Rest. Breathe. Take time off. And be careful of getting sick even when you are feeling good. When your blood counts are low, take it easy. Steer clear of anyone who has a cold or cough. However, don't allow fear of illness grip your life so you become a hermit. Take time to laugh. Find humor in each visit to the doctor, and don't take yourself too seriously. Make up a humorous story about chemotherapy and include it in the Yearbook page that follows. Your story may include Dracula!

Yearbook

Support Among Us

Tara Latta

"God has not called us to see through each other,
but to see each other through." ~Author Unknown

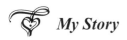 **My Story**

I wrote my story in the following poem entitled, "There is Support Among Us."

It is nothing to fear, it is something to face. With
God on my side, I knew it was grace.
I didn't spend time thinking about the "what ifs."
I have a family, friends, and a career.
I didn't have time for this, but Cancer doesn't care.
So, I adjusted my life to fit Cancer in.
Cancer did not have me, but I had cancer within.
It does not define who I am or the light in my eyes.
I proudly stand and hold my head high.
It has polished my character that shines brightly through.
This was just another test God gave me. I put my
faith in Him to handle my worries.
Cancer did not affect only me. It affected everyone who knows me.
My family, friends, church and office were there for support.
I was showered with love, prayers, cards, food and gifts.
Without cancer, I would have missed out on knowing.
The true meaning of being loved by so many.

How I Got Through It

In the midst of confusion in my whirlwind of life, at age 34 dealing with breast cancer, I found peace and calmness within myself by letting God speak to me. You can find Him all around if you take time to look. I made a list of ten ways I witnessed the peace of God during this tumultuous time in my life.

1. I was at an emotional low point when I got my hair buzzed off. While driving home from the salon I turned the corner and found a series of three signs that made me smile. It was a special message planted there for me. The message said, "Tara...U Make My... (heart) smile."
2. I met friends during my radiation treatment that made me laugh everyday!
3. A group of ladies from my church made me a blanket that is still my favorite.
4. A friend sent me a box filled with socks, candles, a blanket, and chocolate...yum!
5. Letting friends and family cook for me.
6. Reading my Bible. The book of Esther especially touched my heart.
7. While having a garage sale to raise funds for a breast cancer walk, I met some wonderful people in my neighborhood. The amount of friends that donated items was endless. One of my best friends from Colorado even came down to help.
8. Receiving cards in the mail with uplifting messages.
9. My colleagues decorated the entire office in celebration of my full return to work.
10. My husband would leave encouraging messages placed throughout the house and in my purse for me to find.

 ***Action Items***

Are you letting others help you? Are you keeping your eyes open and heart still to watch as God demonstrates His love to you? Start your own list of the ways God has shown up in your life. Even if it seems insignificant, write it down in the Yearbook page that follows. Write a prayer, thanking God for His presence in your life.

❦ *Yearbook*

We Did Everything Together

Barbara Blanton

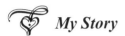 *My Story*

Memorial weekend was a busy one in 2006 as I scurried to see an oncologist. I had just been diagnosed with breast cancer on the left side, and I would require a mastectomy. Fast-forward from that weekend to June 18, when I had surgery. I went to sleep with Stage II breast cancer, and woke up at Stage III. While operating, the surgeon found cancer in the lymph nodes, prompting an immediate removal of those as well. Chemotherapy and radiation soon followed.

My husband Don was by my side and driving me in for treatment. Little did we know, something was happening inside of him also. He wasn't feeling well, and his blood count came back very low. The doctors recommended a bone marrow biopsy.

Two months later, Don was diagnosed with Leukemia. Now, I was driving him. His body didn't respond to treatment, and he was getting weaker and weaker. I was so scared. He was my rock. And then it turned so quickly. We never know what is in store for us.

I wasn't sick one day from my treatment. Nor did I get the fatigue so many women talk about. I was very blessed to be able to take care of my husband during the last days of his life. The following February I finished my treatment. Don was very weak, but he lived long enough to witness me ringing the bell, surrounded by the staff at this clinic, signifying my treatment was finished. For that I am thankful.

How I Got Through It.

We celebrated our 50th anniversary during this journey. Our children were wonderful and very supportive during this time in our lives. They went back and forth between us as we each endured chemotherapy for two different kinds of cancer.

Without faith, family and friends, I don't know how anybody gets through a trying time like this. I sometimes look back on it and wonder how I got through it. Don and I always said, "We can get through anything as long as we've got each other." Don and I had done everything together, and he is by my side even now.

I remember saying to my girls, "Why am I surprised? We shared everything together through our 50 years, so this isn't all that different."

My faith remained strong as I thought, "*whatever will be will be.*" It's all in God's plan. The saying, "God has a plan" was a recurring theme shared by my family throughout this journey. We don't know what His plan is at times, but we keep our faith knowing we will come out of it a stronger person.

Action Items

When I lost my spouse, there were mixed emotions but I didn't question God. My faith is very deep. I believe there is some reason for all of this. I have the feeling I came out of it so I can go forward and do for others. The time I would have spent with Don, I now spend volunteering and helping others who are grieving or going through a crisis in their lives. Don't lose faith!

What is something you will do (now or when you finish treatment) to help someone else? Record your thoughts in the Yearbook page that follows.

Yearbook

Woohoo! Chemo is DONE!!

Kathy Harkey

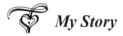 *My Story*

It seems funny that when I started out I thought, "Hmm. I have breast cancer, but I don't really feel sick." The reality of what this means personally comes home each week when they plug you up to some nine or ten bags of stuff that is intended to destroy any cell that is growing. The logic is that it will kill the cancer in the process. It is a test at best, as we all learned, when the first eight treatments failed and my tumors grew. Fortunately, they have even stronger treatments and after six of those, my tumors have shrunk. I can still feel them, but they are smaller. Needless to say at the end of all this, symptoms such as hair loss all over, depleting blood cell counts, fatigue, chemo-brain, and aches all over are just not all that uncommon. Now I think "yes, I feel sick, but thankfully not as sick as many women." I have been able to work after a few days of recovering from treatments. I only had to have treatment for low blood counts this round of chemo. I have fuzz all over my head as my hair starts to grow back. My eyelashes are even growing back.

More importantly, God has been looking over my shoulder this entire time. From the very beginning, I know that God visited me in a dream. I was awakened when a flash of light shocked me, touching my breast in the exact spot of the smallest tumor. I have contemplated this moment now for months. Sure, it could have been a nerve in my body flashing news to my brain that something did not belong, but what I cannot get over is that in my dream, there was a soothing presence by my bedside, and then the flash of light. In my dream I heard the word cancer.

I woke up and shook my husband and told him I had a lump. I could not utter the word cancer then, nor could I utter the word after the first diagnostic mammogram, even though I knew. I waited until after the biopsy because I hoped I was wrong—that the dream was a mistake. But it wasn't. Cancer is a very fearful word.

 ## How I Got Through It.

I had to really come to peace with God and myself. I believe fear is not of God. By focusing on the good things around me and having faith that this is part of God's plan, then it is no longer a fearful thing. That is not an easy task; it is a choice and takes time to resolve, just like it took time to face cancer head on. The message I got in my dream was that no matter what is to come, I had an angel watching over me. I just had to accept that I was on a journey I had not planned. For a control freak like me, it is not easy to let go, but by golly cancer will force you to let go and have faith, or you will be laid low.

This is an amazing journey. It requires looking up and forward and choosing to be positive when many of the things happening to you are not. My journey is not over. I will have a mastectomy soon. After that there may be radiation treatments and some additional chemotherapy after surgery, but at this happy mid-way point, I am celebrating my first victory over this disease.

 **Action Items**

Join me and have a toast of your favorite beverage tonight. Life is good!!

Record your thoughts about your treatment progress in the Yearbook page that follows.

Yearbook

What Cancer Cannot Do

Lucinda West

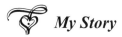 *My Story*

My husband travels for his job, and this particular week he was out of town to lead a conference where pastors from all over the state of Texas came together to learn and worship. Before I got breast cancer, I would often travel with him, and I too would lead conferences for the women. But I had to give up traveling as frequently because of low blood counts and general fatigue. It was emotionally difficult to stay home due to the circumstances, but a choice I felt necessary.

We women often push our own needs aside in order to take care of others. When it is our turn to be taken care of, it is uncomfortable. Unfamiliar. We don't know how to act, say "thank you," or accept what is given to us. Often we are asked, "How can I help?" and we have no response. "Everything is alright," we reply. "No, I don't really need anything." When in reality we are hurting inside and want to be cared for. Maybe we just want someone to talk to—someone to sit with us. Perhaps we need someone to take us to the doctor, or cook a meal, or clean our house, but we just don't want to "impose."

I have discovered through this cancer journey that people get a lot of satisfaction taking care of us cancer patients. They love giving us gifts, bringing us food, and checking in on us. They genuinely want to help! Cancer gives them the opportunity to do something for someone else who has a real need. It blesses them to do it. I have learned to let them.

 *How I Got Through It*

Just about the time I was feeling sorry for myself, wishing I had been able to go with him on this trip, my husband came home carrying a large gift bag. It contained a special gift from a particular pastor's wife who was praying for me in this journey. She lovingly made a lap quilt to remind me that cancer is powerless in so many ways. The colors were a vibrant blue (my favorite color), and it was beautifully hand-stitched with phrases from a famous poem woven throughout the quilted pattern. I had never read the poem until now, and tears came to my eyes as I read the phrases.

> *What Cancer Cannot Do...*
> *(Author Unknown)*
>
> *Cancer cannot conquer the spirit. Cancer cannot corrode faith.*
> *Cancer cannot silence courage. Cancer cannot shatter hope.*
> *Cancer cannot cripple love. Cancer cannot kill friendship.*
> *Cancer cannot stifle laughter. Cancer cannot invade the soul.*
> *Cancer cannot steal humor. Cancer cannot erase memories.*
> *Cancer cannot destroy peace. Cancer cannot erode confidence.*

 *Action Items*

Re-read the poem above, and circle the phrase that stands out to you the most. Are you struggling with love? Faith? Humor? Memories? What can you do this week to beat cancer as it pertains to your phrase? Write about it in the Yearbook page that follows.

🎗 *Yearbook*

When Wigs Fly

DeLann Johnson

*"But they that wait upon the Lord shall renew
their strength, They shall mount up with wings as
eagles, They shall run, and not be weary, and they
shall walk and not faint." ~Isaiah 40:31 (KJV)*

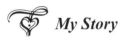 *My Story*

On a Thursday morning after my fourth chemotherapy, I was getting ready for work, and I began to brush my hair. To my surprise it was full of hair! I thought to myself, "My stars. How long has it been since you have cleaned this brush?" Never once did I think that there might be a reason for so much hair! The dreaded day had arrived—the hair was going!

Even though I knew it was going to happen, I just wasn't expecting it this soon, and especially at Easter. My family was very encouraging. The grandkids all wanted to see me in my new wig. I explained that it hadn't been styled yet, but they could get an idea as to what it would look like.

As I paraded in, the girls all said the right things, trying to make me feel good. And then my grandson (bless his heart) just looked at me with this look only a ten year-old could give, and said, "It's okay, but everyone will know you have a wig on." You could nearly hear the three granddaughters' necks snap as they quickly turned to give him a hard look. Of course, he was oblivious to what was wrong. He was just being honest. At a young age, this lesson was evident in the way males and females communicate.

How I Got Through It

I maintained my sense of humor during chemotherapy, and allowed myself to laugh. On Easter weekend we went to Independence, Texas to celebrate the holiday with our friends. We had planned to take family photos with the grandkids before I lost all my hair. That year the wind must have been blowing 100 mph. There was no way we could take pictures at the barn where the party was held, so we drove back to the historical buildings to have a windbreak. I had worked so hard to make my new hair look decent that day, and here the wind was trying to blow it off my head! We were laughing so hard at the thought of my hair literally flying into the wind, it was hard to take the pictures! This laughter enabled me to get through it.

Action Items

While I was doing chemotherapy, one of my daycare mothers, Laurie Smith, sent me a plaque with the verse from Isaiah, and it still hangs on my office wall. I was weary at times. I couldn't run. There were days when I couldn't get up to walk, and yet God helped me through it all and still does as I continue my journey through life. Take a few moments to share your challenges with the Lord in prayer. In the Yearbook page that follows, write about these challenges and how you can overcome them with the strength of the Lord.

Yearbook

Dental Chair

Michelle Martin

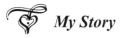 *My Story*

"Thank you God, for putting this beautiful lady in my dental chair right when I needed her!" I was 35 years old when I first felt a lump in my breast. "It couldn't be cancer," I thought. I was only 35 years old. My doctor looked one time with an ultrasound and said, "Yes that's a tumor, let's find out if it's cancer. And there's one more spot I want to biopsy too." I was given the shock of my life. I had breast cancer.

I was so scared and needed direction, but I felt I had none. I decided to pray and ask God for His help and direction in finding the right treatment. I really wanted to go to MD Anderson, but I did not know the first thing about what steps to take. I was asking God to give me guidance and then I fell asleep. I went to work as a dental hygienist early the next morning as I do every work day, only this time I had this heaviness still on my heart, lacking direction in my mind. What happened next can only be described as a miracle.

Providentially, my very first patient that memorable Friday morning was a doctor and radiation oncologist for MD Anderson, Dr. Schlembach. She had just scheduled her appointment with me that week, and it was the first time I had met her. I mentioned my new diagnosis during her cleaning. She sat straight up and told me everything would be fine. She gave me her card and several numbers with instructions on where to send what. Less than a month later I had surgery, followed by six months of chemotherapy, and then six weeks of radiation under her care. I will be forever grateful that God put her in my dental chair that day!

 ## *How I Got Through It*

I realized once again that God directed my path and put several people into my life during my cancer treatment journey to encourage, guide, direct, and support me. He does that! He brings just the right person at just the right time. He brought a doctor, not just any doctor, but a radiation oncologist from MD Anderson specializing in breast cancer, into my dental chair. This experience has helped me many times when things were tough. When I was having my diagnostic mammogram the technician told me, "If they can't tell you what it is, ask for an ultrasound." So I did. And when the radiologist couldn't tell me if it was a tumor or not, I had to self-advocate, convincing him to send me for a biopsy. Grateful for the technicians' insistence and guidance, I decided to pray and ask God for His help and direction in finding the right treatment. By the strength of God I got through it. When the surgeon told me I was wasting my time on a biopsy, but if it would make me feel better he would send me, once again I whispered a prayer to seek God's guidance. All the while God helped me through each step from diagnosing to treatment, by placing the right people in my path at the most beneficial time.

 ## *Action Items*

Think of one person God has placed in your path to help you through this journey, and write about him or her in the Yearbook page that follows. Write something this person said or did that gave you strength or encouragement. When people do cross your way, don't consider it a mere coincidence, but thank God for the divine appointment. Then thank God for them.

Yearbook

It's the Golden Knight!

Lucinda West

 *My Story*

"There is no way I can cover these up without wearing a turtleneck," I thought. I had just gone in for the second "marking" session at the radiation therapist and "held the pose" for 30 minutes while the technicians took x-rays and made more marks with Sharpies on my chest, side, back, and neck. I guessed women who experience radiation in winter would have it a little easier in this respect. While I sympathized with Hester Prynne who bore *The Scarlet Letter*, red and blue marked my neck and chest in semi-circles and polka dots, providing a faint hint of patriotism with a sentiment of Aboriginal design.

I recalled several years ago seeing a lady in a restaurant with little dots prominently displayed on the front of her neck. This memory just came to me, as I had not thought of her since that day. I remembered thinking they were tattoos, and I wondered about their significance. I didn't pry, but I left wondering why anyone would just have a few random dots tattooed on their neck or chest. Now I believe she must have been going through radiation. This shows how ignorant I was about these kinds of things. As a good friend once said, "you've got to live it to learn it."

Radiation was a daily event. After walking our daughter to the bus stop, we hopped on the Harley Davidson and rode to the clinic, got my morning dose of radiation, and then rode home. My radiation oncologist gave a disapproving look and said she would prefer I not…something about fear of broken bones. Radiation makes you very tired, so it's hard to hold onto a bike. She was relieved to hear I am the passenger on a rather large and sturdy touring bike, piloted by my husband. The next day we rode up to the clinic at the same time she arrived. The morning was cool and beautiful, and we had just witnessed a beautiful sunrise. It was her last day working in our clinic and I would be transferred to another radiation oncologist. I showed her the bike, pointed out the safety features, and of course I wear a helmet! She nodded her head and I believe she finally approved.

 ## How I Got Through It

My new radiation oncologist not only approved of our daily motorcycle rides, but supported them as well. In fact, tears came to her eyes when I told her my husband took me on a ride each morning so we could watch the sunrise over Lake Conroe, giving me something to look forward to rather than dread. It helped pass the time. My husband went with me every day, and he gave me inspiration as we rode on the bike together while chatting in our microphones.

We were watching *Wild Hogs* while I was writing this story. As Harley riders, we enjoy watching motorcycle movies, especially before a long trip. Woody (John Travolta) just yelled, "Holy crap! It's the Golden Knight!" encouraging Doug (Tim Allen) to save the day with pizzazz. We laughed out loud the whole evening. This became our new phrase on our ride to radiation, where my Golden Knight would "save the day."

 ## Action Items

Consider how you might make the trip to your radiation appointments fun, rather than a time to dread. Find a routine that works for you. You might stop at your favorite café and purchase a coffee. Buy a special set of songs to listen to just for these trips, or use the time to talk with a friend on the phone. Or, maybe your husband will take you for a ride on the motorcycle. In the Yearbook page that follows, write about something you can do to make the trip to your clinic more fun or interesting.

🎔 *Yearbook*

Message Of Hope

Frances Schlueter

*"Hope is the thing with feathers, That perches in
the soul, And sings the tune without the words,
And never stops at all." ~Emily Dickinson*[8]

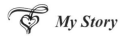 *My Story*

When I was first diagnosed with breast cancer, I was terrified and shocked. My family was very worried about me and I felt like it was my duty to suck it up and not show them how scared I really was. My brave face showed on the outside, but inside I wanted to cry nonstop.

A lumpectomy and radiation therapy was recommend for my type of cancer. I agreed to the treatment plan and worked on numbing my feelings so I could prove how great I was at handling things. The statistics, research findings, and favorable treatment outcomes had little impact on me as I was fixated on the word cancer and its awful reputation.

Everyone waiting for treatment at the radiation therapy center appeared calm and composed, the exact opposite of what I felt. I wanted to cry, but I was wearing my brave face again. All of my efforts were directed toward trying to quell the anxiety that was fighting to surface. My husband's warm hand on my leg reminded me that I was not alone. His love and support calmed me enough to walk to the treatment area for my first radiation session.

Positioned and lying on the table, I closed my eyes and worked on quieting my mind, hoping that tears would not surface. I was told not to move, and I hated the thought of not being able to wipe my tears away. After a few deep breaths and visualizing how calmness would look, I noticed something stirring around in the recesses of my mind; it was the word *hope*. I focused on hope and felt calmness start to enter and spread through me.

Before I knew it, the treatment was finished and I changed back into my clothes, aware of how different and tranquil I felt. That little, four-letter word worked like magic. I reflected on it as I exited to the waiting room to meet my husband. As we left, a wall plaque caught my eye. It said, "Hope." On the drive home, I contemplated how I went from near panic-level anxiety to calmness, all because of one word.

At home, I Googled "hope," searching for meaning and insight. It didn't take long to hit the jackpot—a poem by Emily Dickinson, one of my favorite poets.

How I Got Through It

Emily Dickinson's poem helped me to harness my emotions and find the energy to fight. Through the eyes of hope, I began to see my diagnosis of breast cancer differently, and cancer's reputation started to have a smaller impact in my life. Hope was all around me and it was certainly sitting in the waiting room every time I arrived for a treatment.

 *Action Items*

What or who gives you hope? Write about your source of hope in the Yearbook page that follows. Close your eyes and pay attention as hope whispers in your ear.

Yearbook

Overcomer

Lucinda West

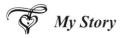 *My Story*

When you're on chemotherapy, doctors of all kinds are more cautious and attentive. Dentists don't want to work on your teeth, the eye doctor delays a vision screening, and oncologists act like guard dogs. Even though you may feel fine, there are times when blood counts are low and you have to be careful of getting an infection... or an illness.

Perhaps it was an undercooked egg, or a virus that everyone else had easily been inoculated to resist, but one day when my blood counts were low, I started throwing up. I was never sick from the chemotherapy, but this particular day (and only this day) I got really ill. I had to excuse myself from a meeting. I lay down for a bit, but the feeling did not subside. It just kept getting worse to the point where I could not even hold down a sip of water. I had a fever as well. My husband called my oncologist, and the nurse said to bring me in immediately. I think the words she used were *"life and death,"* so he was using the right pedal quite effectively.

I remember sitting in my doctor's office, watching the room go black. I said to her, "Dr. Coscio, the room is turning black." She told me later I only said that in my mind, because at that very moment I passed out. She admitted me to the hospital for three days of IV antibiotics. I did get better, and treatment continued. But it was a sobering reminder that this is not just a cold. It isn't just a broken bone. It isn't just the stomach flu or allergies. It is cancer. It is a disease that maims and kills. I suddenly became vastly aware that the poison they were putting into my body to kill the cancer cells was strong and effective, but it also has potentially dangerous side effects which I would need to look out for.

 ## *How I Got Through It*

Around the time of my hospitalization, the words to the following song by Mandisa came on the radio. My face lit up as I listened to the words while tightly embracing each one. Words to this song had been heard many times before, but now I listened with new meaning. It reminded me to keep fighting, and I would overcome this battle.

> *"Whatever it is you may be going through I know He's not gonna let it get the best of you. You're an overcomer. Stay in the fight 'til the final round. You're not going under 'Cause God is holding you right now. You might be down for a moment, feeling like it's hopeless. That's when He reminds you, that you're an overcomer. You're an overcomer."*⁹

 ## *Action Items*

You might want to watch the official music video on YouTube for Mandisa's *Overcomer*, or download it from iTunes. Listen to what the words are saying to you personally, and then reflect on your experience in the Yearbook page that follows. Alternatively, reflect on your feelings toward chemotherapy and take a moment to remind yourself that you will overcome.

🎵 *Yearbook*

_____
_____
_____
_____
_____
_____
_____
_____
_____
_____
_____
_____
_____
_____
_____
_____
_____
_____
_____
_____
_____
_____
_____
_____
_____
_____
_____

Paper or Plastic?

Lucinda West

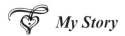 *My Story*

I'm not that old, but I remember when choices were simpler. Phone or mail? White or wheat? Paper or plastic? Life seems so much more complex now. We have twelve types of bread for our sub sandwich and multiple bag options to hold our groceries. Technology has brought us the ability to communicate through email, Skype, Twitter, Facebook, Instagram, and blogs, while snail mail is slowly becoming a virtue of the past. Fortunately for breast cancer patients, technology has also provided more options in the form of plastic surgery.

Just when I thought I had seen every doctor, I was introduced to yet another. I recall the day we met my plastic surgeon for the first time. I was still on chemotherapy. He looked remarkably similar to Jeff Probst, which I thought was appropriate since he would help me to become a survivor. Breast reconstruction is an elective procedure and I would have some tough decisions.

We are blessed to even have this decision to consider. Not too long ago, as late as the 1970s, many breast cancer victims had mastectomies and never considered reconstruction as an option. They suffered in silence, as women didn't talk about their breasts as openly as we do today.

I learned the DIEP flap procedure was my only option. Regardless of the recovery time, I was also told it is worth it. Quality of life and self-esteem in women who have had reconstruction significantly outweighs the quality of life and self-esteem in women who elected not to have the procedure (in a regimented study, according to my doctor). It seems there are many reasons to do it, and fewer reasons not to.

 ## *How I Got Through It*

I wrote this story long before I had the mastectomy or the reconstructive surgery, and now I am resuming my writing on how I got through it. I elected to have the DIEP Flap, which was later followed up with fat grafting, nipple reconstruction and areola tattoo. It took eight months to complete the entire process, as the body needs to rest between each step. I often said that only God can make a perfect breast, but my plastic surgeon comes in a close second!

The recovery was lengthy as anticipated, but I tried not to ruminate about that before I agreed to do the surgery. While I knew it was a choice I could make, I made the decision and never looked back. I feel better about my body, fit better in my clothing, and generally do not have as much tightness in my chest where the breast was removed. My doctor said he was working on my décolletage. While I don't typically wear low cut blouses, it is nice to no longer cringe when I stand in front of the mirror.

 ## *Action Items*

If you are considering breast reconstruction, gather lots of information on options for you. Interview multiple plastic surgeons in your area, or outside your area, and enter the examination room armed with questions. Trust your doctor, and only move forward if you feel comfortable with his or her ability to perform this particular type of surgery. While gathering data, ask women who have had the various types of reconstruction.

What are some of your concerns or fears about reconstruction? Write about your hesitation in the Yearbook page that follows.

✐ *Yearbook*

I Will Walk by Faith

Terri A. Brenon

"For we walk by faith, not by sight."
~2 Corinthians 5:7 (ESV)

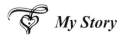 *My Story*

My life was changed in three seconds and five words: "you have inflammatory breast cancer." I was familiar with breast cancer, but had never heard of this kind. I could tell by the look on my doctor's face coupled by the rate at which my tumor grew (three weeks), it was very serious. I immediately kicked into my nurse mode—I had been a psychiatric nurse for many years. I delved into resource, and the more I discovered, the greater my apprehension grew. I felt disbelief and physically sick. I learned that inflammatory breast cancer was a very rare and aggressive form, and the worst kind a woman could get.

I checked out mentally and began contemplating why God would allow such a horrible disease to be in my body. Did I deserve this? Was God punishing me? Why me? I could think of a hundred people 'more deserving' of this ill fate than I was. I knew this would be not only a physical battle, but a mental one as well. I needed to put on my armor for the fight.

The radiologist on call came into the room with more bad news. I had atypical cells in the lymph nodes under my collarbone, which moved me to stage IV. My close friend immediately knew by the look on my face

I had been dealt a major blow. We both wept. We decided to go out to lunch as planned that day, choosing a small table for two, far away from the other patrons.

Two women came in and chose a table right next to ours. I was immediately drawn to the older woman who wore a special hat, and I desperately wanted to hear her story. We approached their table, and I told them what had transpired earlier that day. The woman with the hat told me they had just come from the doctor's office, and she had just been given the news that she was cancer-free. This was her second time fighting cancer and she was previously a stage IV. After she revealed this miraculous information, all that I could hear in my head was God saying to me "I healed this lady of her cancer. What makes you think I can't heal you?" That was a pivotal moment for me. I knew right then and there I would trust God and His plan for me. God had never failed me before. I knew His will was perfect. I immediately let go of all the fear and anger I had. I became particularly fond of 2 Corinthians 5:7 and began walking by faith.

 ## How I Got Through It

With my new outlook on my current situation, I decided to immerse myself in Scripture and start building my "armor" of defense. I placed Scripture on mirrors, cupboards, my dashboard, and any other place where I would be walking. I knew I had to take every thought captive. Trials will come. It is clearly written in the Bible. Without them, I'm not so sure we would be as dependent on God. After recently receiving my zero percent pathology report, I believe I have my answer—God is not finished with me yet. I don't know how much time I have left on this Earth. I don't dwell on that question. As I continue to walk the narrow path, I will keep walking by faith and not by sight.

Action Items

How do you view disappointments and afflictions? Are you willing to trust our sovereign God in the midst of these trying times? I felt my cancer was a win-win situation: If God called me home, I would be free from the pain and illness that plagued my body. There would be no more tears—only joy. On the other hand, if I lived, I would have more time here on Earth to do God's work. Will you do the same? Journal your thoughts in the Yearbook page provided.

Yearbook

No Pain, No Gain

Lucinda West

"He was despised and rejected by mankind, a man of suffering, and familiar with pain." ~Isaiah 53:3

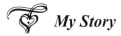 ***My Story***

I had pain in my breast during the hard chemotherapy. It lasted a couple of weeks. Reminiscent of the pain I experienced before I ever started treatment (although not as intense), I feared the cancer was still growing. However, my oncologist was very pleased at my follow-up. She explained that we just killed a whole lot of cancer cells all at once, and this can make one a little tender or cause some pain. She measured the mass and it was shrinking, so that was good news!

Each week, as I geared up for chemotherapy, I said a prayer. I prayed for healing. I thanked God for using the chemotherapy to kill off the cancer. I thanked Him for the pain. I acknowledged this sign that healing was taking place. And I prayed for my infusion nurse who would take care of me that day. "Bless her life, and protect her."

 ***How I Got Through It***

Thursday was my chemotherapy infusion day. I had it on my calendar and it became a part of my weekly routine. I welcomed the chemotherapy into my body, as it was killing the cancer. In addition, I knew I would fall asleep during the heavy doses of chemotherapy, so I planned on an afternoon nap every Thursday during treatment.

The nurses loved to get sweet treats, so I tried to bring a brownie or cookie from our favorite café bakery to give to my infusion nurse each time. It was a small gesture on my part, for such a big thing they were doing for me. I figured it was the least I could do to give back something for the time they spent taking care of me. I never knew who my nurse would be, but they always enjoyed getting the baked goods. Seeing the smiles on their faces gave me something to look forward to, rather than dread, as I went in for my infusions.

 ## *Action Items*

Think of something you can do to help you look forward to your weekly infusions, and consider some things you could do to help your infusion nurse. For example, pray for your nurse. Bring a sweet treat or fresh flowers cut from your garden and give to your nurse.

If ever you are uncomfortable or in pain, let your infusion nurses know so they can help you to be more comfortable. The nurses will provide you with warm blankets and pillows if you ask. That's what they are there for. Don't be afraid to ask!

In the Yearbook page below make a list of things you could do for your infusion nurse, in addition to some ways to help you look forward to your infusion days.

Yearbook

You Are A Survivor

Margaret Looper

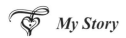 *My Story*

As a volunteer working with cancer patients, the first thing I tell them is, "You are a survivor. You have survived your diagnosis." I silently smile inside as I remember my own survival of the diagnosis several years earlier.

The night before the doctor's visit to get the biopsy report, I felt fear creeping all over my soul. My response was a beautiful prayer of thanksgiving. I felt thankful for being a mother. I gave thanks to God for giving me breasts to nurse my children. I thanked God for the ability to hold my grandchildren close to my chest. I felt grateful for our family. In my prayer, I also asked God to cure me. When I received the results the next day, I felt a peaceful calm, knowing we could handle anything that was before us.

We found our way through the maze of appointments and tests at the "big hospital," guided by a happy, friendly person in a blue jacket. While following a volunteer one day, I thought, "I bet she has never had cancer." When we arrived at our destination, she sat down and visited with me. After chatting with this volunteer (who was a cancer survivor), I thought, "If I get through all this, I could be a volunteer."

How I Got Through It

I got through my diagnosis with a prayer of thanksgiving, and I continue to thank God for what He has done. Thirteen years later, I am free from cancer and the fear of cancer. For the past ten years I have volunteered at M.D. Anderson in The Woodlands, Texas. Once a week, I spend four hours volunteering. Driving home each trip, I review my time spent. I am thankful for those lives who touched my life that day nearly thirteen years ago. I am thankful for the joy of being alive and the opportunity to share that joy with other survivors and the great employees of the hospital.

Several of my family members have also had breast cancer, colon cancer, and leukemia. My niece and I donated blood for studying any relationship between colon and breast cancers. Leukemia took my oldest sister's life, yet I am still at peace. I believe my training as a volunteer in a cancer hospital helped me get through all of my family's cancers.

Action Items

Look for the volunteers at your cancer facility, and take a moment to thank them for their service. You may consider taking a volunteer a baked good, or some other small token of your appreciation. Write about your experience with volunteers in the Yearbook page that follows.

Yearbook

Cancer and The Beatles

Frances Schlueter

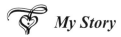 *My Story*

Cancer seemed to dominate my life. My journey through breast cancer and healing covered several years. I would have long periods of treatment and recovery, show improvement and healing, then have a setback or need more treatment. Unable to work or participate in my usual activities, my family was my only anchor to life around me.

I looked for encouragement and inspiration everywhere. I found motivation and meaning in poetry and quotations and would lose myself in the beautiful, soulful words of others. I listened to songs but I tended to listen to the music more than the lyrics, not realizing that songs are poetry put to music. One day, a song's lyrics seemed to speak directly to me and it changed how I listened to music. The message captivated me:

> *"... there will be an answer, let it be. Let it be, let it be, let it be, let it be. Whisper words of wisdom, let it be."*[10]

I listened to the entire song and felt the words sink deep into my heart. I had listened to this song countless times and never heard it speak to me like this before. Later I took a walk, meditating on the message and what I was feeling inside. Cancer had taken away my ability to control what was going on in my life and I had fought this every step of the way. My struggle with the disease lasted for years. My faith had taken a beating. I had so many questions that had no answers. The fear and uncertainty carved a seeming bottomless pit in my soul. I was looking for answers that did not exist, in a world of sickness that was foreign to me. As I walked, I began to realize that true healing would happen only when I took a step in a different direction.

How I Got Through It

I believe God used the song *"Let it Be"* as a reminder that I wasn't in control. Instead, I just had to let go and accept my circumstances. *"Let It Be"* was telling me to let go and accept. It was telling me that I was not alone. There was an answer and it would come when I stopped fighting what I could not change.

I reread the song lyrics with a different set of eyes. Acceptance was the key to winning my fight against cancer and illness. My doctors had reassured me. I had the ability to win the fight, and that's where I needed to redirect my resources. Like it or not, I had to accept that I had a battle to fight. I needed to take down the unnecessary hurdles I had erected.

It took a lot of daily self-reflection to identify when I was waging an unproductive fight, and redirect my energy toward my goal of wellness. I listened to this song several times a day, as a reminder of my intentions. It gave me courage to continue when all I saw was endless obstacles. I learned I needed to face my trials and the feelings that came with them. Victories and setbacks continued to accompany me on my journey before I finally reached my elusive and hard won goal of wellness. My greatest accomplishment was in realizing how much strength I really possessed!

Action Items

Have you heard any songs that seem to be speaking directly to you? Stop and listen. Write about your experience in the Yearbook page below as you hear the tune and pay attention to the lyrics.

❤ *Yearbook*

Beautiful Gifts

Cindy Murray

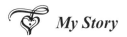 *My Story*

I had a wig on that day I went by Dillard's cosmetics and the lady behind the counter invited me to sit in the chair. My hair just started coming back. I had never had short hair in my life. I'd always had long curly hair. She put makeup on me and turned the mirror so I could look at myself. I started crying. Actually, I was heaving, I was crying so hard. I thought, "This is the first time I've looked pretty in a long time."

The lady said, "You're beautiful. Come back tomorrow and I will do your makeup." What a nice gift she offered me! She gave me a compliment, helped to make me feel attractive again, put fresh lovely makeup on me and offered another makeover session the next day. I was not expecting that! I still remember the kind woman who made my day. She had no idea what was going on.

Aside, my hair came back white, much to my surprise. I am only 55! The doctor said not to put any dye in my hair for a little while, so I didn't. My girlfriends said they loved my hair. Four of my dear friends stopped dying their hair until I could dye mine. What a gift to support me like that.

Many things seem so traumatic when you're going through cancer treatment. But when I look back to the time in therapy, there are so many blessings along the way. What did I learn? To be grateful I have every day.

I am here now and I have experienced many gifts along the way of my cancer journey.

How I Got Through It

Not feeling very beautiful, and feeling like I might die, I made a deal with God. I've never made a deal with God before, but I asked Him to let me live long enough to watch my daughter get married, and see my son do something meaningful with his life. Within that year my daughter was engaged, and within the next year my son graduated fire academy. God let me have the two things I asked Him for, and my perspective changed. From then on I counted everything I got as a bonus. My first grandchild was born four months ago. That was an added bonus. God had more in store for me than what I could imagine. My new perspective keeps me going.

Action Items

I am not suggesting you make a deal with God. But it is helpful to reach out to Him when you are going through a difficult time. No matter how bad it looks right now, set goals to help you look forward to the future. Don't shut the doors in your life. I believe God has a plan for your life. He has more good things in store for you than you could ever imagine.

What is something (or someone) for which you are grateful? Notice the beautiful gifts others have given you throughout your treatment. Now look in the mirror and tell yourself "You're beautiful." Write the words "I am beautiful" as a heading in the Yearbook page that follows. Give yourself a "beautiful gift" today as you list three attributes that you love about yourself.

Yearbook

A New Plan

Janina Stout

"Commit your actions to the LORD, and your plans will succeed." ~Proverbs 16:3 (NLT)

 **My Story**

At this point I am still fighting this crazy cancer.

My husband and I were looking for our new "retirement home." We found one that we liked very much. It was out of state and we were ready to make an offer. But first I had to proceed with my scheduled routine well-woman exam, including a mammogram. Unfortunately something abnormal was found and it would require a biopsy.

I was not worried. A few years back I had a similar experience. But this time was different. I had to have an ultra-sound, and that was scary. My next visit with the doctor, the big "C" word was said for the first time. When I first heard the words breast cancer, it felt surreal. I thought I was having a nightmare, but I was awake. I could not get that it was happening to *me*.

I quickly adapted to this new reality and started on my doctor's action plan. Our retirement home would be placed on hold for now. Scheduling appointments was new for me. I found it both hectic and frustrating. When I called the cancer clinic I had no clue what numbers to press, so I left messages.

I found the waiting to be so hard! I finally got calls back. On my first visit to the oncologist I was told I had stage II breast cancer and I would need a mastectomy. My cancer had tumor markers that were triple positive. So now we moved to another plan. I met with my medical oncologist to discuss my options. They recommended chemotherapy before surgery. They told me they would monitor the response of the tumor to the powerful drugs I was receiving. I am so very pleased to report that my doctor was able to stop the lump from growing with the addition of this powerful chemotherapy regime. The breast tumor is about 40% smaller from what it was when first diagnosed.

Today I only have one more round of chemotherapy to go and then I will have the operation. This time it will be a lumpectomy or segmental mastectomy and not a modified radical mastectomy! I am so grateful for modern medicine and the change in plans for my treatment.

How I Got Through It

I thanked God for my doctors, and all the professional staff I have met along the way. They established a plan to get me through this. I also thank God for my family and friends. Everyone helps to keep me positive and full of hope. My husband and our daughters keep me in their prayers and make sure that I eat healthy food. They also send me care packages with herbal tea and goodies. Our girls keep checking the Internet for new research. Our friends also pray and send me books and best wishes. Knowing people care about me, keeps me positive. I know that with God's help, I will beat this thing.

Action Items

Be open to each plan that unfolds before you. When you are hit with various treatment options, take some deep breaths and ask God to guide your doctors' decisions. Trust your oncologists, who have your best interest at heart and have a lot of knowledge in their respective fields. Take a moment to thank God for the caretakers in your life. Maybe bake them some brownies to take on your next visit. Record your thoughts in the Yearbook page that follows.

Yearbook

Benefits of Bald

Lucinda West

But the Lord said to Samuel, "...The Lord does
not look at the things people look at. People
look at the outward appearance, but the Lord
looks at the heart." ~I Samuel 16:7

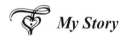 ***My Story***

I admit it; I have grown accustomed to myself as a baldhead. I finished chemotherapy two months ago, and I do have some incredibly fine hair growing back in. It feels like peach fuzz, and I finally quit shaving it off. It's still extraordinarily, very short. However, I have grown to love it!

Ten benefits of being bald:

1. It only takes twenty minutes or less to get ready, from shower to make-up. Sometimes only ten!
2. My head is much cooler when I step outside in the hot, summer air.
3. I don't have to worry about "bad hair days."
4. No more clogged drains. There is no hair to clean up after I use the shower.
5. I can take pictures without my hair flying in front of the camera.
6. No hair to blow in my face, tangle, or creep under my goggles while riding the Harley.

7. It is fun to see the looks on people's faces when I take off my ball cap or motorcycle helmet in public.

8. I don't have to shave (yes, my legs and armpits are bald too).

9. I can wear a wig and no one knows the difference. I chose a wig that resembles my hair. The wig doesn't frizz like my hair, and it only takes a minute to style.

10. I can see my head for the first time in my life.

 ## *How I Got Through It*

I am confident there are others, but you can see there are many benefits to being bald! I could have easily started a pity party at the loss of my hair. It is a loss, and there is a certain grief process that goes along with it. However, I learned to embrace the temporary, new me. I am still me. I am just a little different on the outside. Rather than despising my looks, these thoughts helped me get through this phase of the journey.

 ## *Action Items*

Embrace the baldness. Remember the Lord looks at the heart, not your head. Find something positive and enjoy the, albeit temporary, "new" you. Whether you lose your hair or not, write about your body changes, and how you will cope, in the Yearbook page that follows.

Yearbook

Held

Heather Farris

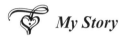 *My Story*

I was thirty years old. I found out I was pregnant the day before I received the diagnosis: breast cancer. I found the lump myself. Because of my age, the lump was not super docile or super aggressive. But, because of my age, they didn't want to take any chances, so my doctor "threw the book at me." The plan: chemotherapy, followed by a lumpectomy in the first trimester, and radiation after the baby was born.

I had always wanted three kids. I already had a son and a daughter, and now I was pregnant for the third time. I didn't know I was pregnant when I did my mammograms and ultrasounds, and that was scary. Still, I felt like God was telling me, "I'm going to give you what you want," and "everything is going to be okay."

The ultrasound just before surgery proved his heartbeat was strong. After surgery, I was jolted into reality as they wheeled me back to ultrasound to determine whether the baby's heart was still beating. That was the longest and most difficult ride I have taken, as a painful thought kept flooding my mind. I whispered prayers for my baby the whole way down the lengthy hallway. *Please, let him be okay.* God answered my prayers. His heart was still beating. He is now five years old and healthy.

How I Got Through It

I prayed—a lot. For whatever reason that defies all logic, I had an overwhelming sense of peace. God was telling me I would be okay. He moved me to a surprising place of exhilaration.

I gripped tightly to the promise conveyed in a song titled "Held" by Natalie Grant. God does not guarantee that everything is going to be great, or that life will be smooth sailing. We will all experience tough times. But we are promised to be held in the Father's arms while we are going through it.

Action Items

Read the following promises of God, and then write a letter to God as you reflect in the Yearbook page that follows.

> *"So do not fear, for I am with you; do not be dismayed, for I am your God. I will strengthen you and help you; I will uphold you with my righteous right hand" (Isaiah 41:10).*

> *"Do not let your hearts be troubled; You believe in God, believe also in me" (John 14:1).*

> *"Peace I leave with you; my peace I give you; I do not give to you as the world gives. Do not let your hearts be troubled and do not be afraid" (John 14:27).*

Yearbook

Goodness Always Follows
a Bad Situation

Rhonda Chenet

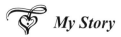 *My Story*

My father told me as a child that goodness always follows a bad situation. Throughout my life, I have constantly tried to live by that saying. In 2008, I was diagnosed with breast cancer and had a bi-lateral mastectomy with reconstruction one month later. I was 48 years old and in great shape, training to run my first full marathon. Exercise had always been a huge part of my life, and continued to be integral to my recovery process.

 *How I Got Through It*

My personal trainer, who is also a dear friend, was going to be a guest speaker at a support group called Breast Friends. She was going to give a talk and demonstration on stretching and exercise after cancer. Several friends and I went along with her to provide moral support and to be her models.

During the evening we broke into small groups and I met a beautiful red haired, blue-eyed woman by the name of Gina. She had been diagnosed with terminal breast cancer that same week. I felt the need to get to know Gina, so I got her telephone number and called her. I asked if I could bring dinner to her and her family and just spend time with her. I did, and I discovered she was a beautiful person inside and out. Over the course of visiting and sharing stories about our families, we became good friends.

Gina had an amazing husband and two lovely sons. I also had a wonderful husband, a son and a daughter. Gina mentioned to me one day that her second son, Mike, would love to meet a nice Christian girl. I said the same about my daughter, Sally, finding a nice guy. We introduced our children, and over the course of the next few months, they fell in love. They were married in July of 2011. Gina was still with us and did a reading at Mike and Sally's wedding. I remember fervently praying that day. God revealed the truth of the saying my father had instilled me. Goodness really *does* follow a bad situation. Two moms, both diagnosed with breast cancer, and through this terrible thing, came love between our two children.

Gina passed away almost two years later, but she gave my family such a wonderful gift: her son to our beautiful daughter.

 *Action Items*

I will always count my blessings and will always focus on the good that follows bad situations. Look for the good things that have happened to you over the course of treatment. Sometimes it may feel like searching for a needle in a haystack of worry, but keep a lookout. Even if it is only one good thing, write about your blessings in the Yearbook page that follows.

Yearbook

Authentic Joy

Peggy Strickland

"Persevere and God will watch over us..." ~Anonymous

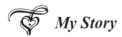 *My Story*

I received a greeting card from a friend and I knew I needed to share a story. The card read:

> There are treasures we find in times of great loss that wouldn't otherwise have been revealed. In the midst of our sorrow we discover the riches of authentic joy in the memories we've made through all of life's seasons, sharing love, laughter, beauty, grace and the anchoring journey of faith.

When I was diagnosed with breast cancer it was only stage one, and I knew I could be helped. I went through six rounds of chemotherapy and 35 rounds of radiation. The diagnosis was not a catastrophic shock to me because I never had many perfect mammograms, starting when I was about 38.

I was touring the radiation center when I met my first doctor. I had visited three oncologists in the area and two felt I should have radiation only. In fact, one of my oncologists followed me because he knew I was going to tour the satellite facility.

How many people have the opportunity of being treated with joy, peace and love from their medical staff? Thanks to my doctors, nurses, coordinators, radiation specialists, massage therapists who freely gave us massages, and new friends in my support group—all the people I know I will never forget—I always felt like I was walking into a safety zone when I entered the cancer clinic.

 ## *How I Got Through It*

I started attending the breast cancer support group a few years later. Each time I went, I saw diverse people with various types of breast cancer, different ages and almost always with a smile and happy to be there—with friends—to tell their story or to hear someone else's story. I applaud all of these women who are so brave. The young ones with small children have a special place in my heart.

I am thankful to all those responsible for supporting us breast cancer patients. They give us the lift that is sometimes hard to reach.

 ## *Action Items*

Locate a support group in your area. If there isn't a support group at your medical center, consider joining an online support group or finding one at another center.

For some additional reading, see James 1:2-4 or James 5:11. Record your thoughts about perseverance and pure joy in the Yearbook page that follows. May you have joy for your spirit, peace for your soul, love for your heart.

Yearbook

The Exclusive Club

Evelyn Goldstein

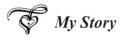 *My Story*

Dripping wet on a late Friday afternoon I heard the words, "I'm sorry to tell you that you have breast cancer...DCIS" (ductal carcinoma in situ is a non-invasive breast cancer, almost exclusively found by mammograms). I carried my cell phone all week waiting for the results of my needle biopsy so I didn't hesitate to jump out of the shower when it rang. The moment I was diagnosed I became a member of an exclusive club. I instantly had something in common with every other person who was diagnosed with breast cancer. No one chooses to be a member of this "club," yet we understand the challenges faced by other members and we support one another.

After I wiped away the tears I called my husband to give him the news. He rushed home to research DCIS on the computer. Although never diagnosed with breast cancer himself, he became an honorary member of the club.

I read two important things about a cancer diagnosis. First, listen to your team of doctors rather than all the other voices that try to advise you. Secondly, once you have a treatment plan in place, you will be able to deal with the fear better. For me, both proved to be true. I listened to my doctors and we soon had a plan in place, alleviating my fears.

One night I was recognized as a member of the exclusive pink ribbon club. My family went to a football game to watch the Houston Texans. It was in

270

October, and it was Pink Ribbon Day. My husband and two of my sons proudly wore breast cancer awareness shirts with pink ribbons pinned to their chests. The stadium was covered in pink and it was amazing to see all of those people supporting our exclusive club. This was my highest point during treatment.

 ### *How I Got Through It*

I have good days and bad days but I'm trying hard to live a healthier lifestyle. It was challenging to get back on track physically after I completed radiation. I signed up for a fitness challenge to raise money for breast cancer research. This motivated me to get back to exercising because I could pick a challenge that is attainable according to my ability.

I took it one step at a time to ensure success, giving up diet soda and drinking fruit infused water all day, making green smoothies, and generally eating healthier. I gained support from my friends as we completed a Bible study together called *The Daniel Plan*. It taught me to eat whole, healthy food and to refrain from eating unhealthy, processed food. My husband has decided to join me. My two youngest sons who live at home are eating healthier and my 22-year-old son has asked me to start making green smoothies for him, too! My sons are also honorary members of the exclusive club, supporting and encouraging me every step.

 ### *Action Items*

There are several action items to consider. Listen to your team of doctors. Remind yourself that once you have a treatment plan in place the fear will subside. You are a member of an exclusive club, and you have many people who understand and are willing to support you in your journey with breast cancer. Reach out to them. As you try to stay on track physically, take one step at a time. Write about one of these action items, or a "high point" in the Yearbook page that follows.

Yearbook

New Life

Gail Mills

*"You make known to me the path of life; you will
fill me with joy in your presence, with eternal
pleasures at your right hand." ~Psalm 16:11*

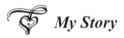 *My Story*

Our daughter was pregnant at the time I was diagnosed with breast cancer, and her husband was in the military preparing to go to Iraq. She and her children were living with us for support during his deployment. Stressful as it was managing our individual concerns, we could have commiserated with each other, sharing our imagined or actual losses while noting our physical conditions and situations. However, rather than swim in the negative stream of thought, we chose to focus on life.

One oncologist noted that some women who go through chemotherapy experience similar symptoms they had when they were pregnant. Although not necessarily based in research, she said she has noticed that those who got morning sickness tend to get sicker with chemotherapy. The lucky women who never got sick while pregnant breeze through chemotherapy more easily. This hasn't been tested, but she has anecdotally witnessed some correlations.

Similarly, my daughter and I had much to talk about. We discussed how symptoms from chemotherapy and pregnancy have a lot of likeness, and how we had things in common: hot flashes, emotions running non-stop and wreaking havoc, some foods smell really good, but then you try to eat them and they taste terrible, etc. To help overcome this obstacle, a friend took it upon herself to come by my house every week after chemotherapy, carrying homemade salsa. This may seem like an unusual act of kindness. However, we appreciated it because salsa was something I could actually taste. We called her the "Salsa Patrol." My pregnant daughter ate it as well, and I'm not sure who ate the most! We were thankful for the friend who thought up something meaningful to do and just did it without restraint.

I kissed my little granddaughter as I was leaving for one of my treatments, and I remember thinking with a smile, "this is what life is all about." She inspired me to keep fighting. A few weeks into treatment, I had chemotherapy in the morning and God gave us a new grandbaby in the afternoon. I had a reminder once again that life is amazing.

How I Got Through It

I continued to be amazed as I went through the remainder of my treatment regime, which consisted of a mastectomy, radiation, and then on to DIEP flap reconstruction. When I woke up in the ICU after my DIEP flap, I had a new breast. But it was more than just a breast. It was the beginning of a new life! I remember when they put the Doppler on my newly formed breast to listen; I could hear the blood swish through the connected blood vessels. The sound was reminiscent of the swish I had heard with my own kids and grandkids when their mothers received ultrasounds during various pregnancies. I immediately thought of it as the sound of new life. Focusing on life helped me to press on and get through it.

 *Action Items*

Life is amazing. Look for evidence of new life around you. Thank God for living things: the birds in the air, the grass in your lawn, your lungs that give you the ability to breathe, or whatever comes to your mind. Write a prayer of gratitude for new life in the Yearbook page that follows.

Yearbook

Never Alone with Cancer

Alice Stone Thomas

"God has said, 'Never will I leave you; never will I forsake you.'" ~Hebrews 13:5b

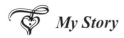 *My Story*

I prayed all the way home from the radiologist's office. "Dear God, please let the biopsy be benign."

In my heart I heard Him reply, "I will never leave you nor forsake you."

"Excuse me, Father," I continued, as I switched lanes and tried to see through tears. "Can you cook my meals, drive me to surgery, and be with me for four-hour chemotherapy treatments? Not to mention all the radiation treatments?"

Silence.

As a single woman, I thought I had nobody to take care of me. God would be there in spirit, but what about the work that needed to be done? Soon God showed me differently. He provided the people and showed up in their presence. He was there as I underwent chemotherapy; each of my three children swooped in and cared for me. One daughter drove me to chemotherapy treatments. Another daughter is a nurse and came by each day after work to check my vitals and perform other nursing duties. My other daughter took a week off from work in New York to fly home and care for me.

Every day, colleagues from the high school where I taught visited me carrying food, flowers, and encouragement. Students brought gifts and their parents sent encouraging emails. Neighbors and church friends offered to take me to treatments, cook my meals, and bring in my mail. My sister sat with me during one of the chemotherapy treatments. My son-in-law, Steve, stayed with me during a round of chemotherapy.

 ## How I Got Through It

During the treatments when I was weak and sleeping so much, my family and friends visited me regularly and phoned daily. Through the 30 radiation treatments, they continued to support me. Through the words and actions of my family and friends, I kept hearing God say, "I will never leave you nor forsake you." Now I know He never will.

During my chemotherapy, I would often wake up at 2:00 a.m. I viewed this as an opportunity to write a book I have been thinking of writing for a long time. I began writing a book entitled *Leaving Your Legacy of Family Faith*. Writing the book kept my mind occupied, and gave me a sense of purpose while I was undergoing treatment. It's a story about the legacies my relatives left to me. I wanted my grandchildren in New York to know about their mother's family in case I was not here to tell them. I finished the book in about one month and had it ready when their mother (my daughter) came from New York to take care of me during round three of chemotherapy. God's presence played an important role in this legacy.

Action Items

When you are facing a life-changing situation, in whom do you trust to save you? What is your sense of purpose? Ponder these questions and read Hebrews 13:5 again as you reflect your thoughts and feelings in the Yearbook page that follows.

Yearbook

Faith Benefits The Journey

Marti M. Syring

"Have I not commanded you? Be strong and courageous.
Do not be afraid; do not be discouraged, For the Lord
your God will be with you wherever you go." ~Joshua 1:9

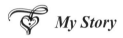 *My Story*

I have three sons and a daughter. The reactions of my children upon hearing that I had breast cancer were as unique as their individual personalities. While each of my children was encouraging in his or her way, and I appreciated their concern, they could not fully relate to my situation. So, I reached out for additional support through the clinic. After my second visit with the surgeon, I read a flyer in the lobby regarding a breast cancer support group. When I attended the group, I found a bunch of women eager to support me in my journey with breast cancer. All of them had already experienced the journey, or were still in their journey. This group could relate.

The first night I attended the group various members shared their stories and what helped them through it. Several ladies mentioned scriptures from the Bible, and this was encouraging. One lady quoted my favorite verse from Joshua. As I listened, I realized I was becoming stronger emotionally, and at that moment I began to rely on the Lord and the Holy Spirit. My spirituality grew throughout my cancer journey. I learned that I could do anything with the Lord's help. I am more than a survivor. I am a thriver!

How I Got Through It

One of the greatest things someone shared with me during this time was a paraphrased scripture, "Have faith. Do not be afraid, for the Lord Jesus has suffered all of your pain and hard times and He will be with you through all of this. When you feel down and out, think of Him (the greatest physician) and you will feel relief." I followed this advice numerous times and it benefitted me greatly.

Many things helped me get through the journey including: blessings from priesthood men in my church, prayers of family, friends, coworkers, and church members, faith on my part, focusing on the pain the Lord Jesus suffered for me on the cross of Calvary, staying active, learning all I could about my diagnosis, family and friends coming with me to the treatments, and the great doctors and medical personnel.

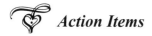

Action Items

Where is your faith for healing? Who is the great physician that has ultimate power? When you feel down and out, focus on Him and you will feel relief. Also, as you walk through this journey, find support in those individuals who will encourage you and relate to your illness. Be encouraged by each individual's response, recognizing they have a unique, God-given personality and it is acceptable for them to respond in different ways. Reflect on these thoughts in the Yearbook space provided.

🖋 *Yearbook*

Trust Your Inner Voice

Christine Potter

*"Don't let the noise of others' opinions drown
out your own inner voice." ~Steve Jobs*

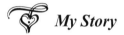 **My Story**

Between work and dealing with my mother's recently diagnosed breast cancer, it had been difficult to make time to see the doctor. After examining my breast, the doctor assured me that a fibroid cyst, not cancer, was causing the pain. "You are just feeling like this because your mother has breast cancer." I still felt uneasy, so I insisted. I needed to be sure. Consequently, the doctor ordered a mammogram. Results: I am my mother's daughter. It was invasive ductal carcinoma of the right breast.

Fourteen years later, I am 43-years old. I decided to finally have reconstruction and get rid of the prosthesis. Everyone, including my husband, told me it was crazy and not to do it. Unnecessary surgery is dangerous. He said, "Have you forgotten all of the problems you encountered when you had cancer?"

Despite his advice, I had the surgery. As I lay on the gurney prior to surgery, I almost changed my mind. Instead, I said a quick prayer and felt I should proceed. My last thought before the surgery was, "I can't wait to wake up with a tummy tuck and two perfectly balanced boobs." Then I woke up.

"Excuse me!?" I still had the same old boob, no pain in the stomach, and nothing on the right side of my chest except a bandage with a drain. I said to myself, "I must be dreaming; I'm still in surgery." Dr. Chambers (my heroine and surgeon) came to check on me. "I don't think this was our plan was it?" I asked. She explained that she found a recurrence of breast cancer on my breastbone while she was removing tissue for the reconstruction. Results indicated it was ER+, PR-, invasive ductal carcinoma. Once again I faced surgery and chemotherapy, but this time, no radiation. The cancer was too close to where they treated me before.

A few years later, I kept getting an irritating feeling on my left side. I thought it was scar tissue but decided to see my doctor anyway. Unfortunately, the doctor reported cancer again, and recommended surgery. "How did this happen?" I thought. "I don't have any breast tissue left!" Despite that the results showed triple-negative invasive ductal carcinoma. So, I said good-bye to the prospect of beautiful boobs. Instead I said hello to more surgeries, radiation, chemotherapy, and prostheses for both breasts.

 ## How I Got Through It

Each time I had a feeling something wasn't quite right in my body, I persisted. Each time, I was right. No matter what others said (such as, "don't worry so much," or "don't get the surgery,") I felt like I had to do it. The voice in my head, the quiet voice of the Holy Spirit, this conviction, saved my life on more than one occasion. I am thankful I didn't allow the voices outside my head to stop me from pursuing what I knew was the right thing to do each time.

 ## Action Items

Advocate for your own body. If you feel a lump or something is not quite right, demand a scan or biopsy, or whatever it takes to allay your fears. We know our bodies better than anyone else. After all, we have lived with our bodies for our entire lives! Get to know each little nook and cranny so you will be aware when something changes. More importantly, don't live every day in fear. Write about the external noise and your inner voice in the Yearbook page that follows.

Yearbook

April Fools

Vicki Massaquoi

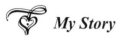 *My Story*

It was April 1ˢᵗ when I received my diagnosis of breast cancer and I vividly recall wondering, *"Are you fooling me?!"* It was surreal. My doctor patted me on the shoulder as he handed me a tissue and encouraged me to cry. But I didn't cry. I told him, *"God's got this. It's alright."*

But the words fell on my own deaf ears, because it wasn't all right. In fact, it was all wrong—terribly, terribly wrong. It took three weeks to gather the strength and courage to tell anyone, including my family. First, I told my oldest daughter, and then, my mother.

When I told my daughter I had breast cancer, she reacted, *"Momma, it's alright. You're not gonna die. You're gonna make it."* She started making plans to go with me to all my appointments. She spent time with me and cared for me. During one visit to the doctor she actually had me laughing as she said teasingly, *"Momma you're gonna be a 57 year old woman with breasts sticking straight up in the air!"* Now that's a word picture. Seriously though, my daughter's positive attitude boosted my spirits. My daughter has made a difference in my life. She prompted me to go get my nails done, get a wig, and take care of myself. With her support I didn't feel alone in the battle.

Next I told my mother the news, and she said the same thing, *"It's going to be alright."* She was positive, but she is also a lot like me. She held her true

288

feelings inside though not quite able to mask her fear. I could tell on her face she was worried. She had already lost two sons that year and a third had just finished chemotherapy. Still she remained strong, and encouraged me to do the same.

I waited until one week before my surgery to tell my co-workers I had cancer. I had never missed a day of work. Suddenly I was leaving early to go to the doctor. They were beginning to wonder what was wrong. When I finally shared my story, the words stuck in my chest and I couldn't cough them out. It was hard to admit that I wouldn't be there, that I was taking time off, and I would be going through treatment. I saw a light bulb over their heads as they listened. Now they understood what I had been going through. A caring but conflicted look became evident on their faces. They hated to hear it, but they wanted to be supportive. Once again I heard those familiar words, *"You're going to be alright."*

 ## How I Got Through It

Every time I talked about it—with my daughter, my mom, or my co-workers—I got emotional. In fact, I still get emotional almost two years later. I finally decided to attend a cancer support group, which helps a lot. As I talk to other women and listen to their stories, it gets easier to share my story. It's still hard to shake the emotional turmoil and sadness I feel inside at times, but I manage to keep a positive mental attitude. I still hold all my emotions inside, rather than showing it on the outside. I still get dressed up and make myself look nice. I don't want to look like I'm sick. This helps me get through it.

 ## Action Items

The people closest to you and caring for you can make a difference. Share your story. Talk about how you feel. Start with one or two people who are closest to you. The more you tell your story, the easier it will be to tell. If you are afraid to talk to others, you may need comfort and strength before you do. Read Psalms 23. When you read it, know that God is the Good Shepherd and we are His sheep. Take a moment to ask Him to dwell (live) inside of you, and write about your experience in the Yearbook page that follows.

Psalm 23 (KJV)

The Lord is my shepherd; I shall not want. He maketh me to lie down in green pastures: He leadeth me beside the still waters. He restoreth my soul: He leadeth me in the paths of righteousness for His name's sake. Yea, though I walk through the valley of the shadow of death, I will fear no evil: for Thou art with me; Thy rod and Thy staff they comfort me. Thou preparest a table before me in the presence of mine enemies: Thou anointest my head with oil; my cup runneth over. Surely goodness and mercy shall follow me all the days of my life: and I will dwell in the house of the Lord forever.

Yearbook

I Fought! I Won!

Joy Cabanilla

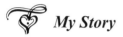 *My Story*

My mammogram was negative and six weeks later while doing a self-breast exam I found a lump. No one wants to hear "You have cancer." The shock of that sentence – and when it finally wears off surface – the unbelief, the "Why ME?" The anger, the sadness, and finally...the depression.

Trying to be strong for loved ones is harder than being strong for myself. That's the easy part. When I'm alone with all my thoughts, I can break down and cry—a lot. It is exhausting to stay positive with my family and friends when in the back of my mind I'm fighting for my life. At the same time, my friends and loved ones struggle to be strong for me. I have seen my family's eyes when they see me. They try to smile and be strong, even though I know it has taken a toll on them.

To be honest, I did not want to do anything. I did not want to do chemo, surgery or radiation. I did not want my life to be disrupted. I kept asking, "WHY?" Why would anyone want to disrupt her life? Do I have a choice??

After much contemplation I accepted the treatment plan that was given to me. My thoughts were, "I will do all I can with what my medical team suggests because ***I WANT TO LIVE.***" And I began each day to fight to see another day, to fight to see my future grandchildren, to fight to be "normal" again.

All I know is that there is a reason for each journey and challenge. I don't know the answers, and I may never know. I do know that I can look back and be thankful that I had the strength because of God, His angels, my family and friends, and my medical team.

I FOUGHT. I WON. So can you, Pink Sisters and Brothers!

 ## *How I Got Through It*

While I was fighting this battle, I watched funny shows and movies. Something about laughter soothes the soul and gives a positive outlook on life. Also, when I found out I was diagnosed, I put Post-it notes on my bathroom mirror with affirmations of healing. That helped me a lot! I have *many* quotes from others, or self-awakening quotes, but the one that stuck to me most from the start of my journey was found on a t-shirt. It said, "Hey Cancer, you messed with the wrong woman." I took a picture and have it on my bathroom mirror.

 ## *Action Items*

Think of quotes or affirming words that you can rely on day by day. Record your thoughts in the Yearbook Page that follows. After you finish writing, put some Post-it notes with various words of affirmation around your house.

Yearbook

Ring the Bell!

Lucinda West

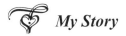 *My Story*

I came away from the clinic feeling a bit overwhelmed. It was a good feeling, joyful and relieving all at the same time. I knew at this moment God had answered our prayers. After completing my 33rd and final dose of radiation, I was officially a survivor! My son and several MD Anderson staff joined me for the bell ringing ceremony. This was a sacrifice for my son, as he had worked late the night before and I had an early morning appointment. Unexpected tears came to my eyes as we closed this chapter of life. I felt so blessed by all the prayers, thankful for the words of encouragement, and overwhelmed by the number of people who have walked steadfastly through this journey with us.

Admiral Irve Charles Le Moyne is credited for starting this tradition. According to his obituary, he was the nation's highest-ranking Navy Seal and a founder of the United States military joint special operations command. He came to MD Anderson for treatment of advanced head and neck cancer in 1996. Nearing the end of his treatment, he told his doctor he wanted to ring a bell when the job was done, as was tradition in the Navy. They installed a bell with a plaque at MD Anderson in downtown Houston in his honor, and the bell ringing tradition spread from head and neck cancer patients to all cancer patients, from the downtown clinic to other satellite offices, and continued to spread to other hospitals and treatment centers.

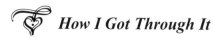

How I Got Through It

As I thought about ringing the bell while lying on the radiation table from day to day, it gave me hope that I would successfully finish this race. It was something to look forward to. The bell was a symbol of completion. Success. A period at the end of a very long chapter. Life! Finally here, tears welled up in my eyes. I was filled with emotion words can't describe. I didn't know the story of Admiral Le Moyne when I read these words on the plaque out loud, but I thank him for starting this tradition.

> *"Ring this bell*
> *Three times well*
> *Its toll to clearly say:*
> *My treatment's done*
> *This course is run*
> *And I am on my way!"*

Action Items

Consider a way to celebrate the day you finish your treatment. If your clinic does not have a bell, perhaps you can share this story with them and ask them to gather around you as you ring a bell, signifying your treatment is done. Or, invite your friends and family to gather around you on the day you come home from your final treatment. As you anticipate completing treatment, list some ideas for celebration in the Yearbook page that follow. If you will have ongoing maintenance treatment, consider how you might celebrate each new phase, year, month, or day of life.

✿ Yearbook

_____

_____

_____

_____

_____

_____

_____

_____

_____

_____

_____

_____

_____

_____

_____

_____

_____

_____

_____

_____

_____

_____

_____

_____

_____

_____

_____

My Mentor Kathy

Pamela J. Schlembach

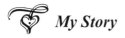 *My Story*

Kathy and I worked together in the 1970's. I was a radiologic technologist trainee and she was a seasoned nuclear medicine technologist. She mentored me in so many ways. She was a young, cute, petite woman with a strong work ethic and good patient skills. Kathy instilled in me a desire to further my education. She gave without expectations, was a confidant to many, a peacemaker, a teacher, and truly my favorite employee. By the early 1980's, Kathy was in her 30's and a mother of two rambunctious, blond-haired, little boys. I had since married, moved away, and began to pursue a higher education. I thought of her often and would stop by the hospital just to see her for a mini mentoring session on life whenever I was in town.

I received news that several months after the birth of her second child, she had a solid mass resembling cancer in her breast. At the time it seemed impossible. She was too young to have this disease. No one in her family had breast cancer. She had even breastfed. But to everyone's surprise, her breast biopsy revealed a high-grade invasive ductal carcinoma. I do not remember the details of her stage but I remember we were all concerned for her. Unfortunately, her cancer returned a few years later. The staff she worked with took up a hospital wide collection and sent her and her husband on a once-in-a-lifetime dream vacation.

I remember visiting Kathy after she was diagnosed with metastatic breast cancer. She was bald, walking with a limp, but still hopeful, continuing to mentor me about life. As we walked with a stroller down her busy street, Kathy shared how she was hoping for the best but preparing for the worst. She planned to enter a clinical trial. I listened intently, tears streaming down my cheeks, as my mentor shared more of life's saddest, toughest, and bravest lessons. My sweet Kathy, my mentor whom I loved, was dying, and there was nothing I could do. I left her that day knowing it would probably be the last time I would see her alive. She was gone within the year.

Kathy taught me about how to live even when you are dying. She was determined to enjoy her time with her family and friends. I am so grateful to all of the "Kathys" out there who have helped make progress in cancer treatment by furthering the knowledge of how to treat and cure this awful disease by their participation in clinical trials. I am grateful for the tenacity of the human spirit to keep going and to have hope.

 ## How I Got Through It

Kathy taught me life lessons that I would not fully understand or appreciate until many years later. I never dreamed on our last walk together that I would someday become an oncologist and treat the very disease that took her young life. But there she was, mentoring me in lessons for my future. Thank you hardly seems adequate for the way she touched my life, and the lives of others, but I guess that is what real mentors do. They prepare us with lessons and principles for the unknown path ahead, impacting future generations, sometimes without even knowing it. Even now, Kathy mentors me. I wish I could tell her how much she did for me; I hope I too can be a mentor others.

 **Action Items**

Do you have a mentor? If so, take a moment to recall one or two lessons he or she has taught you about life. As you complete this book and move forward in your journey with breast cancer, consider how you might become a mentor to others. Record your thoughts in the Yearbook page that follows.

Yearbook

Notes

1   Sorensen, S. & Geist, L. (2007). Praying through cancer: Set your heart free from fear. Thomas Nelson.

2   Throughout this book we chose to use the feminine pronouns since breast cancer is most commonly attributed to women. Several men have also contributed stories as caregivers of women with breast cancer. This is not to negate any males with breast cancer. Men with breast cancer, as well as their family members, may also benefit from reading and journaling through this book.

3   Dwyer, W. W. (2001). There's a Spiritual Solution to Every Problem, 2nd ed. Harper-Collins.

4   Jeremy Camp wrote this song during his honeymoon with his first wife Melissa Lynn Henning-Camp, who was diagnosed with ovarian cancer and passed away just four months after their wedding day. If he can sing while experiencing that hardship, I can walk by faith as well.

5   With increases in technology, the number of lymph node survivals has greatly increased since I was diagnosed with cancer, and survival rates vary according to each person's individual diagnosis and treatment.

6   Morgan, J. (2001), The Red Sea Rules, Nashville, TN: Thomas Nelson, Inc.

7   ©2006 Debra Jarvis for National Public Radio, Inc. Transcript from NPR news report titled "Sorry About the Cancer, How's Your Hair?" was originally published on All Things Considered on August 31, 2006, and is used with the permission of NPR. Any unauthorized duplication is strictly prohibited.

8   Dickinson, Emily. The Collected Poems of Emily Dickinson. New York: Doubleday, 1997.

9   Overcomer Lyrics. (n.d.). Lyrics.net. Retrieved February 4, 2015, from http://www.lyrics.net/lyric/29793114

10 Lennon, John, Paul McCartney, George Harrison, and Ringo Starr. Let It Be. The Beatles. Parlophone, 1987. CD.

Made in the USA
Middletown, DE
07 January 2022

58035698R00194